SET APART

a 6-week study of the beatitudes

Jennifer Kennedy Dean

NEW HOPE
PUBLISHERS

Birmingham, Alabama

New Hope® Publishers
P. O. Box 12065
Birmingham, AL 35202-2065
www.newhopepublishers.com

New Hope Publishers is a division of WMU®.

Library of Congress Cataloging-in-Publication Data

Dean, Jennifer Kennedy.
  Set apart : a 6-week study of the Beatitudes / by Jennifer Kennedy
Dean.
     p. cm.
  Includes bibliographical references and index.
  ISBN 978-1-59669-263-3 (sc : alk. paper)
  1. Beatitudes--Textbooks. 2. Beatitudes--Criticism, interpretation,
etc. 3. Sermon on the mount--Textbooks. 4. Sermon on the
mount--Criticism, interpretation, etc. I. Title.
  BT382.D37 2009
  226.9'306--dc22
                          2009018139

ISBN-10: 1-59669-263-4
ISBN-13: 978-1-59669-263-3

N104132 • 0909 • 7.5M1

DEDICATION

To my sons and my beautiful daughters-in-law

Brantley and Caroline
Kennedy and Sara
Stinson and Stephanie

And to the always fresh memory of my husband, Wayne. Dad extraordinaire.
Still influencing our lives, though absent from our sight. Our golden one.

NOTHING GOLD CAN STAY.
—ROBERT FROST

TABLE OF CONTENTS

PREFACE

Welcome to this study. In this study you are about to discover the freedom to which God has called you and the joy that is yours.

I love writing Bible studies. I write them for me. When you read my studies, you are eavesdropping on what God is saying to me. And I welcome you! Isn't the Scripture a never-ending treasure trove? It never ceases to amaze me that a topic about which I think there can surely be nothing left to say, suddenly unfolds new and fresh revelation and insight. Living Word, breathing on our hearts and minds the breath of life.

I had a wonderful time researching and writing *Set Apart*. I pray that the challenge of holiness engages your heart fully and the power of the Holy One becomes your experience.

The first week is longer and more intensive than the subsequent weeks. I tried to pare it down, but it is foundational. We must understand these principles before any of the rest of the study will make sense. So, don't be overwhelmed during the first week. Just take your time. It is longer, but I think that it is necessary and that you will find the effort worth your time.

If you don't have the *Set Apart* DVD Leader Kit, consider getting it. You will find helpful materials, including an appendix to this book in which I explore Romans 6–8 in more depth. I think you will also enjoy "Heart's Cry," the song that Roxanne Lingle and I wrote for this book. Included in the kit, you will have the words, the music, and even a music video. There are also some promotional materials to help you get the word out about your study.

Blessings,

Jennifer Kennedy Dean

INTRODUCTION

BE HAPPY

Human beings were created with a compelling drive to be happy. God intentionally created that compulsion, embedding it in our nature, as surely as He created everything else about us. Every manufacturer of goods exploits the need for happiness in advertisements and enticements to buy his product. Observe the barrage of ads that assault your senses and clamor for your attention. They all have the same underlying message: This is what you have been looking for. This will make you happy! If only your teeth were whiter or your hair were shinier or your car were faster or your house smelled like cinnamon…then you would be happy! Creators of such advertisements have spent untold millions on market research, looking for the hot button that will make the audience purchase what they are offering. Apparently, their research leads them to the same conclusion time after time. People are in a desperate search for happiness. They will go to any lengths to find it.

Observe the enticements to happiness that come in your mailbox, through all kinds of electronic media, and on billboards. Notice that advertisers are finding more ways to make their promises: grocery carts, restroom stalls, hotel key cards, product placements in movies and TV shows, and so forth. A never-ending barrage of promises. Why do advertisers spend so much money on touting their products? What does that tell you about their research?

God wants you happy. He created you so that your desire to be happy surpasses all other needs. People will forfeit anything they have—health, finances, relationships, dignity, whatever it takes—if they are convinced that happiness will follow.

God created you with this need for happiness because He intends it to be His opening into your life. Your desire for happiness is to be the catalyst that opens your life to Him. This very need drives you to His heart.

Look at these declarations from the Psalms, representative of the eternal message from God's heart to His people. Joy and pleasure may be treated as synonyms for happiness. Highlight words that represent happiness.

You have made known to me the path of life;
you will fill me with joy in your presence,
with eternal pleasures at your right hand.
—Psalm 16:11

The precepts of the LORD are right, giving joy to the heart.
—Psalm 19:8

Surely you have granted him eternal blessings
and made him glad with the joy of your presence.
—Psalm 21:6

Satisfy us in the morning with your unfailing love,
that we may sing for joy and be glad all our days.
—Psalm 90:14

Light is shed upon the righteous
and joy on the upright in heart.
—Psalm 97:11

Does God promise happiness?

Would He promise something He was not willing to provide?

Would He promise something He did not desire His people to have?

God's Kind of Happiness

Yes, God wants you happy. He *"delights in the well-being of his servant"* (Psalm 35:27). His anointing is an anointing with *"the oil of joy"* (Psalm 45:7). However, He alone knows the key to your happiness. He alone created in you that urgent drive to find happiness, and He alone is its fulfillment. Apart from Him, the search for happiness leads to emptiness.

We all have things we think would bring happiness. If only this would happen. If only that would change. If only I had this. If only... Sometimes the worst thing that happens to a person is for her to get her "if only"—only to discover that even then, happiness eludes her.

When the need that should have turned us toward God is instead turned toward something outward in the world, then happiness is an elusive quest. Happiness is a mirage. The closer you get to it, the farther away it proves to be. Those things in the world that promise happiness only meet the outside edges of the need. Instead of having the need met and fulfilled, the need becomes overpowering, driving, compelling. Instead of being freed from that need by having it eternally satisfied, we instead become enslaved to that need because it is forever unmet.

When we look for happiness outside of God, external circumstances become the focus. If we can keep our circumstances under control, if we can surround ourselves with possessions and relationships and situations that make us feel significant, then maybe happiness is possible. The problem is that the externals will not stay in order. You will be caught in a trap. Your work will never be done. It will wear you out.

God wants to free you from that need that compels you to manipulate and manage everything and everyone around you. He wants to bring such happiness to your innermost being that you'll be free from the fear and the emptiness that keep you focused on externals. God has designed you for true happiness. Until you find that happiness for which you were created, you will be unsettled.

If God created you with the need for happiness and if God wants you happy, then surely He has provided the way for you to be happy.

> "Creatures are not born with desires unless satisfaction for those desires exists. A baby feels hunger: well, there is such a thing as food. A duckling wants to swim: well, there is such a thing as water....If I find in myself a desire which no experience in this world can satisfy, the most probable explanation is that I was made for another world. If none of my earthly pleasures satisfy it, that does not prove that the universe is a fraud. Probably earthly pleasures were never meant to satisfy it, but only to arouse it, to suggest the real thing."
> —C. S. Lewis, *Mere Christianity*

The desire for happiness is meant to awaken your desire for God and His kingdom. His key to happiness is unexpected and disconcerting. It turns every quest for happiness upside down. The pursuit of happiness, it turns out, is the pursuit of holiness.

In this study, you will discover eight secrets to happiness. Happiness has a new definition in God's kingdom. In the everyday language of that kingdom, the word for "happy" is *blessed*. Blessedness is the true form of happiness you are seeking. Blessedness is a solid, steady, immovable contentment that is rooted inside you rather than being a fleeting emotion that is based on events outside you.

God's Kind of Happiness Comes from God's Kind of Holiness

> *As obedient children, do not be conformed to the former lusts which were yours in your ignorance, but like the Holy One who called you, be holy yourselves also in all your behavior; because it is written, "You shall be holy, for I am holy."*
> —1 Peter 1:14–16 (NASB)

Did your mother ever say to you, "Pretty is as pretty does"? Let me borrow from that phrase and turn it around. Holy does as holy is.

Set Apart

Holiness is a concept steeped in Jewish thought from the nation's birth. Israel was a holy nation, God's own people, set aside for His purposes. A little group of people—a family that grew into a nation—separated out from among the nations of the earth to be God's possession. Beginning in the book of Leviticus we see God defining *holy* through word and parable and edict and ritual. What God took from among the common things and set aside for His use was declared to be holy. *Holy: set apart for God's use.* Something or someone became holy because God said, "From now on, this is holy to Me." Having made something or someone holy by declaration, He then set about cleansing that person or object so that they were holy in practice.

In the Old Testament, which is our primer or our picture book, God gives us the picture of holiness in various ways. The Sabbath was declared holy (Genesis 2:3). It was to be set aside for God's purposes only. In the accounts found in Exodus and Leviticus of the tabernacle structure and furnishings, each article is declared holy—to be used for no purpose other than that which God had assigned it. Having declared each article holy, He then gave instructions for its cleansing, thereby making it pure and holy in experience. *"Then you shall take the anointing oil and anoint the tabernacle and all that is in it, and shall consecrate it and all its furnishings; and it shall be holy"* (Exodus 40:9–10 NASB).

The priesthood was chosen from among the people and given a specific role within the holy nation. They were a holy tribe within a holy nation. They were to perform only the tasks that God assigned them. They were set apart for God's use. *"Then you shall bring Aaron and his sons to the doorway of the tent of meeting and wash them with water. You shall put the holy garments on Aaron and anoint him and consecrate him, that he may minister as a priest to Me"* (Exodus 40:12–13 NASB).

These examples are just a glimpse of the picture of holiness painted throughout the Old Testament. The definition never varies. God conferred holiness upon something, then worked that holiness out in practice. To be holy meant to be set apart for God's use—whether person, animal, day, or instrument. When God declared something holy, from then on, holiness defined it. God doesn't share. If He's set something apart, it is His and His alone. All His.

God brings that same definition of holiness right into the New Testament and makes it the centerpiece of the new kingdom. You are holy because God has declared you so, has cleansed you with the eternal blood of the Lamb, and is now working out that holiness. 1 Peter 1:14–16 says to be holy *"in all your behavior."* Why? Because *"You shall be holy for I am holy."*

I'm going to imagine that you have always read that sentence as if it is a command. Go ahead. Read it aloud and read it as if it is a command. How do

13

you feel about such a command? Pretty intimidating, isn't it? Wildly unrealistic, right?

Now, read it again. This time, read it as a promise.

He has set you apart. He has called you aside. He has given you a purpose and assigned you a destiny. He has written across your life "Holy unto the Lord." This is His promise to you: *"you shall be holy."*

Set Apart

WEEK ONE

DAY 1

BLESSED ARE YOU

Please read Matthew 5:3–10.

In this passage, the Greek word translated "blessed" is *makarios*. It is a Greek word translating the Hebrew word Jesus most likely used when He gave this sermon in real time. Jesus and His contemporaries spoke Aramaic, a language closely aligned with Hebrew, but used Hebrew words and phrases for very Hebraic concepts. The Hebrew language had an expression that can be translated, "Oh the blessedness of …!" This was an expression commonly used by the rabbis and sages to introduce concepts similar to those Jesus was stating in the Beatitudes. This structure was familiar to Jesus's audience.

The Hebrew word that the Greek word *makarios* is interpreting is *esher* and it has the sense of congratulations. The Hebrew root, *ashar*, means to be straight, or even, or level, and it implies to move forward or advance. It implies stability and success (*Theological Wordbook of the Old Testament*).

Looking again at the Greek, we can gain further nuance to our understanding of the word *blessed*. The word *makarios* was used by secular Greeks to describe the state of their mythical gods, who had everything they needed and were completely satisfied all the time.

Behind the original usage of this word by the Greeks lay the idea that the gods were blessed in themselves, unaffected by the outside world. This condition of blessedness is ascribed to the gods, for instance, by writers such as Homer and Hesiod, who spoke of the gods as distinct from men who are liable to poverty and death. Thus, one general conclusion we can draw is that the word *makarios* originally meant that state that is neither produced nor affected by outside circumstances, but is intrinsic within. This is the underlying principle in the use of the word in the Septuagint and the New Testament.

—Spiros Zodhiates, *The Beatitudes*

So, pulling it all together, the phrase Jesus likely used, which is translated into English as *blessed*, was a commonly used Hebrew phrase of congratulations. So I believe the implied meaning refers to the kind of deep-seated joy and happiness that is rooted on the inside and not altered by circumstances on the outside. Blessedness in this context implies that all one's needs are supplied and all desires fulfilled.

Blessed means the quality of life that God Himself possesses. You were created to live in a state of blessedness, and it is established through holiness. *"But just as he who called you is holy, so be holy in all you do; for it is written: 'Be holy, because I am holy'"* (1 Peter 1:15–16). Blessedness is the quality of life only found in God Himself, and He wants to impart it to you. Blessedness is the by-product of holiness, the essence of who God is. He is holy. We need no other word to describe Him. Because He is holy, and because He has set you aside and declared you His own, you are holy by declaration, becoming holy in experience. We are "becoming by grace what He is by nature" (from the Orthodox Creed, "Sanctification").

How would you describe the difference between happiness, as we typically define it, and blessedness?

_____

_____

Do you recognize some "if onlys" in your own life? If only..., then I would be happy.

_____

_____

_____

What externals (circumstances, people, things) do you try to manipulate and manage? What do you think motivates you in this endeavor?

_____

_____

_____

🜚 🜚 🜚

The Law of the Covenant

Before we go forward in our study of the Beatitudes, let's look back at a foundational passage from the Old Testament. Having freed His people from slavery in Egypt, God gave Moses what we call the Ten Commandments. Moses stood at the foot of Mount Sinai and repeated what God had spoken to Him about the laws to which His people should adhere. God explained to Moses that these ten directives were the keys to experiencing His blessing on their lives.

Then Moses went up to God, and the Lord called to him from the mountain and said, "This is what you are to say to the house of Jacob and what you are to tell the people of Israel: 'You yourselves have seen what I did to Egypt, and how I carried you on eagles' wings and brought you to myself. Now if you obey me fully and keep my covenant, then out of all nations you will be

my treasured possession. Although the whole earth is mine, you will be for me a kingdom of priests and a holy nation.' These are the words you are to speak to the Israelites."
—Exodus 19:3–6

The commandments Moses gave the people are recorded in Exodus 20. It was understood that following these principles would cause the people to live in the blessings of God. When they lived by these laws, their behavior would prove them to be set apart from all other nations. The meaning was: "Blessed are you if you have no other gods before Me."

"I am the Lord your God, who brought you out of the land of Egypt, out of the house of slavery.

"You shall have no other gods before Me.

"You shall not make for yourself an idol, or any likeness of what is in heaven above or on the earth beneath or in the water under the earth.

"You shall not worship them or serve them; for I, the LORD your God, am a jealous God, visiting the iniquity of the fathers on the children, on the third and fourth generations of those who hate Me, but showing lovingkindness to thousands, to those who love Me and keep My commandments.

"You shall not take the name of the LORD your God in vain, for the LORD will not leave him unpunished who takes His name in vain.

"Remember the sabbath day, to keep it holy.

Six days you shall labor and do all your work, but the seventh day is a sabbath of the LORD your God; in it you shall not do any work, you, or your son or your daughter or your male or your female servant or your cattle or your sojourner who stays with you.

For in six days the LORD made the heavens and the earth, the sea and all that is in them, and rested the seventh day; therefore the LORD blessed the sabbath day and made it holy.

"Honor your father and your mother, that your days may be prolonged in the land which the LORD your God gives you.

"You shall not murder.

"You shall not commit adultery.

"You shall not steal.

"You shall not bear false witness against your neighbor.

"You shall not covet your neighbor's house; you shall not covet your neighbor's wife or his male servant or his female servant or his ox or his donkey or anything that belongs to your neighbor."
—Exodus 20:2–17 (NASB)

Set Apart

These were the behaviors that God desired in His people. If they could follow these commands, exhibit these behaviors, then they would live their lives under the blessing of God, fully supplied and lacking nothing. These are the actions that would prove them to be God's holy people, set apart for His purposes.

How did the people respond to these commands? *"And all the people answered with one voice and said, 'All the words which the Lord has spoken we will do!'"* (Exodus 24:3–4 NASB). We will *do*. We will perform. We will behave.

Their experience soon showed them that they could not obey, even though they intended to and wanted to and tried to. They could not produce the behaviors that God required.

The Law of Sin and Death

Why did God give the Old Testament law, knowing that His people could not keep it? What purpose did the law serve?

First, through the law, we learn what sin is, and we learn that we sin. *"Through the law we become conscious of sin"* (Romans 3:20). *"Indeed I would not have known what sin was except through the law"* (Romans 7:7).

Second, the law is to serve as our training ground, leading us to grace. *"What, then, was the purpose of the law? It was added because of transgressions until the Seed to whom the promise referred had come"* (Galatians 3:19).

"Before this faith came, we were held prisoners by the law, locked up until faith should be revealed. So the law was put in charge to lead us to Christ" (Galatians 3:23–24).

To protect us from ourselves and our self-defeating impulses and inclinations, the law was given. It gave us the standard toward which to aspire. By outlining behaviors that would bring a person into God's blessings, the law curbed some of our destructive tendencies and kept us safe until the fullness of faith could be revealed in Christ.

The school of law is essential to discovering grace. God created us with a will. He must prove to us by experience that our own will, no matter how determined and well-intentioned, cannot make us holy. We are impotent to keep the law and save ourselves by our right behavior. This is a reality that we must learn by experience.

Even though we are saved by grace and grace alone, once we enter that relationship and are born into the kingdom, most of us try to live in the kingdom by law. We put forth our best efforts and fail. We work harder and fail. Then we work really, really hard. And fail. We feel all the law's condemnation. We feel discouraged and unworthy. We miss the kingdom's promise of happiness because we are trying to live in the new kingdom by the laws of the old kingdom.

This is something that we don't understand until we experience it. You might be still in the school of law right now. You might feel discouraged and unworthy. If so, be encouraged. Grace is the law of the new kingdom, and you are about to encounter its transforming power.

What is the law's purpose?

_____

_____

How does God use the law to grow us into grace?

_____

_____

The Law of the Kingdom

As Moses had in a previous generation, now Jesus stood on a mountain and pronounced the law of God's kingdom. We call His pronouncement the Beatitudes and the Sermon on the Mount. Reminiscent of Moses setting forth the covenant law, Jesus proclaimed the kingdom law. Moses's declaration dealt with behavior. Jesus's declaration dealt with the heart that would produce the behavior. Jesus took the emphasis off of outward actions and put it squarely on the heart.

When Moses had finished his presentation, the people were determined to perform well and be confident in their ability to do so. In contrast, those who heard Jesus's words that day surely realized immediately that He was requiring something of them that was impossible for them to produce.

Jesus laid out the conditions for happiness, and they were beyond the ability of human beings. Then Jesus began to explain that the law of the old covenant, which was outside of His people and could only *command* their behavior, had been transformed into the law of the kingdom, which is inside the heart and can *empower* their behavior.

Did God change His mind about the law and about how He wants His people to live?

_____

Highlight the words that describe the law:

So then, the law is holy, and the commandment is holy, righteous and good.—Romans 7:12

The righteous requirements of the law.—Romans 8:4

The law describes the righteousness of God that He wants to reproduce in His people. Has anything about the content of the law changed?

_____

_____

God's definition of what holiness looks like has never changed. The conduct He set out in the Ten Commandments is still His commandment. These behaviors will keep us safe and whole and uncontaminated by the world. These commands are God's first grace to us.

WEEK ONE

DAY 2

THE JESUS LAW

When King Jesus gave His inaugural address, the Sermon on the Mount, He opened it with the Beatitudes. Then He proceeded to embellish His introductory statements and to illustrate them in more detail. As He moved through His sermon, He explained:

> *"Do not think that I have come to abolish the Law or the Prophets; I have not come to abolish them but to fulfill them. I tell you the truth, until heaven and earth disappear, not the smallest letter, not the least stroke of a pen, will by any means disappear from the Law until everything is accomplished. Anyone who breaks one of the least of these commandments and teaches others to do the same will be called least in the kingdom of heaven, but whoever practices and teaches these commands will be called great in the kingdom of heaven. For I tell you that unless your righteousness surpasses that of the Pharisees and the teachers of the law, you will certainly not enter the kingdom of heaven."*
> —Matthew 5:17–20

Jesus makes clear that God did not change His mind and throw out the law. The law describing the moral conduct of our lives (by this I mean the Ten Commandments, not the ceremonial laws) will never change. But something did change. A seismic change occurred between the Old and New Covenants, between the law of the Old Covenant and the law of the kingdom.

The Relocation of the Law

The difference between the Old and New Covenants is not the content of the law, but the location of the law. In the Old Covenant, the covenant of law, the law was on the outside.

The law on the outside could command holiness, but could not produce holiness. The only power the law on the outside could wield to control behavior was the fear of punishment. It could not change the heart that produced the behavior. It could control behavior with limited success through fear of consequences, but it could not eradicate the inclination toward sinful behavior.

Examine these statements that describe the difference between the Old Covenant and the New Covenant. What does the Scripture say sets the New apart from the Old?

"The time is coming," declares the LORD, "when I will make a new covenant with the house of Israel and with the house of Judah. It will not be like the covenant I made with their forefathers when I took them by the hand to lead them out of Egypt, because they broke my covenant, though I was a husband to them," declares the LORD.

"This is the covenant I will make with the house of Israel after that time," declares the LORD. "I will put my law in their minds and write it on their hearts. I will be their God, and they will be my people. No longer will a man teach his neighbor, or a man his brother, saying, 'Know the LORD,' because they will all know me, from the least of them to the greatest," declares the LORD.

"For I will forgive their wickedness and will remember their sins no more."
—**Jeremiah 31:31–34**

"I will give you a new heart and put a new spirit in you; I will remove from you your heart of stone and give you a heart of flesh. And I will put my Spirit in you and move you to follow my decrees and be careful to keep my laws. You will live in the land I gave your forefathers; you will be my people, and I will be your God. I will save you from all your uncleanness."
—**Ezekiel 36:26–29**

We'll explore two questions from here: What is the law on the inside called? How does the law on the inside work?

DAY 3

WHAT IS THE LAW ON THE INSIDE CALLED?

Here is the way the Apostle Paul succinctly states our new condition under the New Covenant, life under the law of the kingdom: *"For sin shall not be your master, because you are not under law, but under grace"* (Romans 6:14).

Imagine this statement written on a sheet of paper: *You are under law.* What would it mean to be "under law"? It means that the law is in charge of you. It means that you are accountable to the law. It means that the law is your authority. We have already noted that the law is good and righteous and holy. There is nothing wrong with the law. To be under law is to be under God's protection. It is a demonstration of His love, caring for you until grace is revealed.

Now, in your imagination, look again at the statement: *You are under law.* Watch as a big red editor's pen crosses out the word *law* and inserts the word *grace. You are under grace.* I want you to say that phrase out loud, but change the inflection you usually give the words. Say it like this: "You are not under law, but you *are* under grace."

Grace has taken over the position of the law. Grace is now going to do what the law was assigned to do but was inadequate to accomplish. *"What the law was powerless to do ... God did ... in order that the righteous requirements of the law might be fully met* in us, *who do not live according to the sinful nature but according to the Spirit"* (Romans 8:3–4). We will look at that passage in more detail later, filling in where the ellipses are. But right now I want you to see the basic statement Paul made. *"What the law was powerless to do"*—make us holy, empower our behavior, change our hearts—*"God did, in order that the righteous requirements of the law might be fully met."* Where are the righteous requirements of the law to be met? *"In us."* We are set apart to be a display of God's splendor.

How did God accomplish in us what the law could not? Look again at these words from Ezekiel and from Jeremiah:

> *"This is the covenant I will make ... ," declares the* LORD. *"I will put my law in their minds and write it on their hearts. I will be their God, and they will be my people.*
> —Jeremiah 31:33

> *"I will give you a new heart and put a new spirit in you; I will remove from you your heart of stone and give you a heart of flesh. And I will put my Spirit*

in you and move you to follow my decrees and be careful to keep my laws.... You will be my people, and I will be your God."
—Ezekiel 36:26–29

Do you see the parallel language?
"I will be their God, and they will be my people."
"You will be my people, and I will be your God."

Let me show you the first time this statement is made.

"Therefore, say to the Israelites: 'I am the LORD, and I will bring you out from under the yoke of the Egyptians. I will free you from being slaves to them, and I will redeem you with an outstretched arm and with mighty acts of judgment. I will take you as my own people, and I will be your God. Then you will know that I am the LORD your God, who brought you out from under the yoke of the Egyptians. And I will bring you to the land I swore with uplifted hand to give to Abraham, to Isaac and to Jacob. I will give it to you as a possession. I am the LORD.'"
—Exodus 6:6–8

One of the foundational principles of the Jewish interpretation of the Torah (Old Testament) originated with a rabbi named Hillel the Elder, 110 B.C. to 10 B.C. His methods of interpretation influenced all rabbinic study of the Old Testament Scripture and is evident in the way New Testament writers interpreted the Old Testament. One of Hillel's seven principles of interpretation was *gezerah shavah* (literally, "cut equally"). It means, essentially, when the same wording is used in two different texts, the same meaning is to be applied in both places.

In these three passages (Exodus, Jeremiah, Ezekiel) you see an example of *gezerah shavah*. All three passages have the phraseology *"I will be your God, and you will be my people"* or a minor variation. The foundational first mention is in Exodus 6:7; these are the words that declare the people of Israel set apart of God's purposes. This is the covenant promise God makes with His people.

The significance of the four cups of wine to be served at Passover comes from this passage in Exodus. Each cup celebrates one of the *"I will"* statements from Exodus 6:6–8.

- Cup of Sanctification: *"I will bring you out from under the yoke of the Egyptians."*
- Cup of Judgment or Cup of the Plagues: *"I will free you from being slaves to them."*

- Cup of Redemption: *"I will redeem you with an outstretched arm and with mighty acts of judgment."*
- Cup of the Kingdom*: "I will take you as my own people, and I will be your God."* (This is God's covenant promise to Israel. This promise signifies that the people will be His kingdom, set apart from all the nations of the earth.)

You can see that the phrasing *"I will be your God, and you will be My people"* was well entrenched in Hebrew thought as a reference to God's covenant and kingdom. Every time that phrasing appears, it will be referencing covenant and kingdom. In each of the passages we are now observing, the covenant-kingdom phrasing is used. Clearly, each is referencing a covenant that establishes a kingdom.

God promises a new covenant for a new kingdom. The New Covenant will be inscribed, not on tablets of stone, but on the tablet of the heart. Pay particular attention to the words from Ezekiel: *"I will remove from you your heart of stone and give you a heart of flesh."* The original law was engraved on stone tablets by the finger of God. When a stone is engraved, the markings are cut into the stone and become one with it. When God engraves His law on your heart, His law becomes one with your heart. Your heart changes. Your heart is set apart for one purpose: to contain God's law.

> And so the heart in which God gets His way, and writes His law in power, lives only and wholly to carry that writing, and is unchangeably identified with it.
> —Andrew Murray, *The Two Covenants*

Now look at the words of Jeremiah 24:7, noticing the phrase that identifies it as talking about covenant and kingdom: *"I will give them a heart to know me, that I am the LORD. They will be my people, and I will be their God, for they will return to me with all their heart."* In the New Covenant for the new kingdom, He will give His people a heart that knows Him. In Jeremiah 31:34, He states the same thing in these words: *" 'I will be their God, and they will be my people. No longer will a man teach his neighbor, or a man his brother, saying, "Know the LORD," because they will all know me, from the least of them to the greatest,' declares the LORD."*

In the kingdom of God, all kingdom dwellers get a heart transplant. The new heart knows God, and His law is its heartbeat. Look what God says will change: *"And I will put my Spirit in you and* move you *to follow my decrees and be careful to keep my laws"* (Ezekiel 36:27, author's emphasis). He will be the power in you moving you to follow His decrees and be careful to keep His law. The law will not be outside of you, commanding you. The law will be inside you; empowering you. Cleansing you. Perfecting you. Doing on the inside what it could not do on the outside.

Grace Full

Do you remember where we started this discussion? Paul's statement, *"You are not under law, but under grace,"* tells us that grace is what God calls the law on the inside. Grace is a power that works mightily in you, bringing you to holiness.

Look at this statement Paul made about grace.

But by the grace of God I am what I am, and his grace to me was not without effect. No, I worked harder than all of them—yet not I, but the grace of God that was with me.
—1 Corinthians 15:10–11

Do you see Paul identifying grace as a power working in him, changing him, and empowering him? Highlight phrases in those verses that refer to grace as active power.

What the law demands, grace provides. Under the rule of grace, everything that God demands of you, He provides for you. Under the rule of grace, the law that once condemned now empowers. *"For the law was given through Moses; grace and truth came through Jesus Christ"* (John 1:17–18). When grace was revealed, the law was filled up to its fullness. The law was only a one-dimensional picture of God's heart. Not inaccurate, but incomplete.

Grace certainly means the unmerited favor of God. Grace—God's action on our behalf—is what brought us into the kingdom in the first place. But many times we think only of grace as that which brought us to salvation and do not realize that the same grace works in us as an active force to sanctify us and empower us.

Before we move on to the second question about the law on the inside, take the time to solidify what you have just learned.

What is the difference between the Old Covenant and the New Covenant in terms of the law?

_____

_____

_____

Why does God move the law from the outside to the inside?

_____

_____

What is the result of having the law on the inside?

_____

_____

What do you understand this to mean: *"You are not under law, but under grace."*

_____

_____

_____

How Does the Law on the Inside Work?

Go back once more to our pivotal statement: *"For sin shall not be your master, because you are not under law, but under grace"* (Romans 6:14). Under law, sin masters us. But under grace, we are freed from sin's mastery.

Paul, in Romans 6, is explaining the transition from being bound to a law on the outside to being freed by a law on the inside. It is a detailed discussion. For our purposes, we will look at only a few points. Some of you may be interested in a more in-depth discussion of these concepts, and you may download a careful treatment of the passages in Romans 6–8 from my Web site. This material is also included on the *Set Apart* DVD Leader Kit.

When Paul talks about being free from the law, he makes some people nervous. In his day, as in ours, some people are afraid to be free from the law, thinking it will lead to sin. Paul addresses the obvious question: If I am free from the law, then are there any constraints on my behavior? Will I not exercise my freedom by breaking the commands of the law? (Romans 6:1–2) To our surprise, we find that grace is better able to keep us from sinning than the strongest allegiance to the law could ever be.

Remember, the law in itself is not bad. In fact, it is good, righteous, holy, and true. Part of the law is its good and righteous commands; the other part is the penalty for not keeping its good and righteous demands. The law on the outside has only one power for controlling behavior: fear of punishment.

Grace has two components. It is receiving from God what we don't deserve because of Christ. It is also the power of God operating in us to produce a righteous life. Much to our surprise, His power and life indwelling us is *more effective* at producing right behavior than was the law with its demands and penalties.

Let me explain it this way: The laws of the United States prohibit murder. The law lays out a penalty for murder. I have never committed murder, nor will I ever. However, the reason I have never committed murder has nothing to do with a law on the books; it has to do with a law in my heart. There is a law in my heart against murder that makes it impossible for me to commit murder. Though a law on the books exists and that law is good and right, I am not "under it"—it does not hold me in check. In fact, I never even think about the law against murder! I spontaneously obey it. A law on the books against murder is unnecessary for controlling my behavior.

Now, suppose that the law against murder were not in my heart. Would a law on the books, with its accompanying penalty, keep me from murdering? Fear of the consequences probably would inhibit me to an extent. But, should the right circumstances present themselves, I might commit murder.

Let me tell you how it is with another law of the land that is not in my heart. There is a law on the books, with accompanying penalty, against driving faster than the speed limit. That law, I have to confess, is not in my heart. Most of the time the threat of fines causes me to obey the law. But if the circumstances are right, I can rationalize my way around the law, and I can convince myself that I probably won't get caught and then have to pay the penalty if I do.

Now, which is the more effective at controlling my behavior? The law on the books or the law in my heart? When Paul tells us that we are not under the law, but under grace, he is saying that we are free from the law on the books, the written code, because of the law in our hearts.

Grace will produce a deeper obedience than law produces. For example, there is no law of the land to prohibit bitterness. The written law imposes no punishment on me for being angry and nursing a grudge. However, there is a law in my heart against bitterness. Because of grace—the law in my heart—I cannot nurse anger and allow bitterness. Because the law is in my heart, bitterness and anger CANNOT be at home there. This is what Jesus was explaining when He said that He came to take the law to its fullness. *"Do not think that I have come to abolish the Law or the Prophets; I have not come to abolish them but to fulfill them* (fill them full)*"* (Matthew 5:17, author's amplification added). He explained this statement in Matthew 5:21–22. The law, He explained, prohibits murder. Grace, however, prohibits the inner attitude that produces murder. The depth of the law, the law of grace, requires a depth of holiness that flesh cannot, under any circumstances, produce on its own. A person can keep himself from murdering by using will-power; a person cannot keep himself from being angry by using willpower. The law of grace requires an inner power, the power of the law on the inside.

So the conclusion is that the law as a written code to be followed is good. It is right. But it is powerless. The law as indwelling power is the one and only means by which consistent righteous living can be produced.

Do you see how much more effectively the law inside me can change my behavior than the law outside me? As we learn more about the power of the law in us, creating the heart that produces holy behavior, we will find that God's law, once impossible to obey, becomes progressively impossible to disobey.

True happiness—what Jesus calls blessedness—becomes the tenor of our lives as we learn that happiness comes through holiness. Some people wrongly think of grace as the freedom to be as sinful as they want to be. But grace is the freedom to be as holy as you want to be. Grace is not a license to behave as you desire, but a power that works in you to recreate your desires and progressively make holiness your natural inclination.

Want to be happy? Seek to be holy.

Think about the law that is engraved on your heart. What are some attitudes and behaviors that the law in your heart prohibits?

_____

_____

_____

Are there some attitudes and behaviors that you used to be able to engage in, but with maturity in the Spirit, you are no longer able to engage in freely?

_____

_____

_____

WEEK ONE

DAY 4

HOW DOES THE LAW GET INSIDE?

The law is the foundation of God's Word. God's Word is embodied in Jesus. He is the Living Word, and so the Living Law. When the law is moved to the inside, the question is not, What is the law? but Who is the law?

> *In the beginning was the Word, and the Word was with God, and the Word was God. He was with God in the beginning. Through him all things were made; without him nothing was made that has been made. In him was life, and that life was the light of men....*
>
> *The Word became flesh and made his dwelling among us. We have seen his glory, the glory of the One and Only, who came from the Father, full of grace and truth.*
> —John 1:1–4, 14

The Word who was from the beginning is the living and present Jesus, who has taken up residence in you and in me as His followers, making us His home. The power of the law on the inside is the very power of Jesus. He is the Vine, we are the branches. His life flows through us now, in all His power and with all His holiness.

"I am the vine; you are the branches. If a man remains in me and I in him, he will bear much fruit; apart from me you can do nothing" (John 15:5). Does a branch have any life in itself, any power on its own? No. A branch has only the power and the life of the vine. A branch through which the vine's life is not flowing is fruitless deadwood. The vine's life produces the fruit. The branch displays the fruit. When fruit grows on the branch, it is the outward expression of the inner life. What life flows through the branch? You can tell by the fruit.

All earthly things are the shadows of heavenly realities—the expression, in created, visible forms, of the invisible glory of God. The Life and the Truth are in Heaven; on earth we have figures and shadows of the heavenly truths. When Jesus says: "I am the true Vine," He tells us that all the vines of earth are pictures and emblems of Himself. He is the divine reality, of which they are the created expression. They all point to Him, and preach Him, and reveal Him. If you would know Jesus, study the vine. How many eyes have gazed on and admired a great vine with its beautiful fruit. Come and gaze on

the heavenly Vine till your eye turns from all else to admire Him. How many, in a sunny clime, sit and rest under the shadow of a vine. Come and be still under the shadow of the true Vine, and rest under it from the heat of the day. What countless numbers rejoice in the fruit of the vine! Come, and take, and eat of the heavenly fruit of the true Vine, and let your soul say: "I sat under His shadow with great delight, and His fruit was sweet to my taste."
—Andrew Murray, *The True Vine*

Meditate on John 15:1–8.

"I am the true vine, and my Father is the gardener. He cuts off every branch in me that bears no fruit, while every branch that does bear fruit he prunes so that it will be even more fruitful. You are already clean because of the word I have spoken to you. Remain in me, and I will remain in you. No branch can bear fruit by itself; it must remain in the vine. Neither can you bear fruit unless you remain in me.

"I am the vine; you are the branches. If a man remains in me and I in him, he will bear much fruit; apart from me you can do nothing. If anyone does not remain in me, he is like a branch that is thrown away and withers; such branches are picked up, thrown into the fire and burned. If you remain in me and my words remain in you, ask whatever you wish, and it will be given you. This is to my Father's glory, that you bear much fruit, showing yourselves to be my disciples."

Write down what you see as Jesus's life flowing through you right now. What are the characteristics embodied in Jesus's life that you are seeing in your own life today? Give the Holy Spirit time to reveal new perspectives to you.

_____

_____

_____

The life of Jesus is communicated to us by His Holy Spirit. We are indwelt, filled with, saturated with, flooded with His Spirit. The very life of the living and present Jesus, transfused into us by His Spirit, is the law on the inside.

With that as reference point, let's continue to see from Scripture how the indwelling life of Christ is far more effective in producing holiness than the law on the outside.

The Transforming Power of Grace

In his letter to the Romans, Paul addresses the difference between having the law on the outside and having the law on the inside. He describes the struggle of a person who is trying as hard as he can to keep the law.

> *We know that the law is spiritual; but I am unspiritual, sold as a slave to sin. I do not understand what I do. For what I want to do I do not do, but what I hate I do. And if I do what I do not want to do, I agree that the law is good. As it is, it is no longer I myself who do it, but it is sin living in me. I know that nothing good lives in me, that is, in my sinful nature. For I have the desire to do what is good, but I cannot carry it out. For what I do is not the good I want to do; no, the evil I do not want to do-this I keep on doing. Now if I do what I do not want to do, it is no longer I who do it, but it is sin living in me that does it.*
> —Romans 7:14–20

The law is good, and the person Paul is describing wants very much to keep the law and be holy. But the law has no power to offer, other than the fear of punishment.

Having made that point, he then introduces into the discussion another law.

> *So I find this law at work: When I want to do good, evil is right there with me. For in my inner being I delight in God's law; but I see another law at work in the members of my body, waging war against the law of my mind and making me a prisoner of the law of sin at work within my members.*
> —Romans 7:21–23

Paul is saying, if I may paraphrase, "There's another law at work in me—the law of sin. This law operates like the law of gravity: when you drop something, it falls to the ground. It has to. It has no other choice, because it is subject to the law of gravity. Well, you see, there is a law of sin at work in me. I have to obey it. I have no other choice. It's a law."

What bad news! Paul is describing what it's like to have your soul (mind, will, and emotions) and your spirit (God's dwelling place) out of alignment. The goal is that your spirit-life will be expressed through your thoughts, your will, and your emotions; but in the scenario Paul has outlined, the soul is responding to a pull from outside—the familiar voice of law. This is not how God intends for your life to be. He intends for your thoughts, your desires, your feelings, and your actions to be in harmony with your new nature, the life of Christ in you. He intends for you to be integrated—your actions lining up with your desires.

As long as your enemy, the devil, can keep you focused on your inability to be righteous, he can keep you from discovering that the law of grace is at work inside you. He can keep you from fully realizing that you are dead to his power and that you are now alive to God's power. He can keep you from realizing that the very life of Jesus Christ is in you and that you can let that life flow through you, breaking every old sin pattern that he has left behind. He can keep you from knowing the law of the Spirit of life.

An Overriding Law

Paul says, *"What a wretched man I am! Who will rescue me from this body of death?"* (Romans 7:24). Paul is saying, "I'm dragging around dead weight. I can't get anywhere. My efforts are frustrated at every turn." And here Paul makes the first step toward freedom. He says, "Who will rescue me?" Finally, he sees that his best efforts at keeping the law cannot free him from sin's hold.

Go back to the law of sin. Paul said that the law of sin must be obeyed, just like the law of gravity must be obeyed. Then, he introduces yet another law, the law of the Spirit of life. *"Through Christ Jesus the law of the Spirit of life set me free from the law of sin and death"* (Romans 8:2). He says that one law sets him free from another law.

Imagine that I am holding two inflated balloons. One is inflated with the air from my lungs. The other is inflated with helium. They look the same. There's no way to tell by appearance which is which.

Now, imagine that I take the air-filled balloon and I throw it. It falls to the ground. Why? Because it is subject to the law of gravity. So no matter how hard or how far I throw it, it will always fall to the ground eventually.

Imagine that I then take the helium-filled balloon and I throw it. It doesn't fall to the ground. Instead, it floats! Why? Is the law of gravity no longer in effect? Of course, the law of gravity is just as strong as it has ever been, but this balloon is subject to another law, the law of buoyancy. When the law of buoyancy is in effect, it overrides the law of gravity. When the law of the Spirit of life is in effect, it overrides the law of sin.

For my two balloons, what made the difference? One was filled with the same air that fills the earth. I breathed in earth-air and blew it into the balloon. It was subject to the law of gravity. The other balloon was filled with something else. It was filled with something that defied the pull of gravity. What are you filling your life with? What are you taking in? Are you filling your life with flesh-thinking? Flesh says, "I can do it. I can be good if I'll just try hard enough. I'll put forth more effort." Or are you filling your life with spiritual understanding? "Christ in me, my only hope."

As you consider Paul's words, what is it that the person trying to follow the law on the outside is missing?
___ **Desire**
___ **Motivation**
___ **Knowledge**
___ **Passion**
___ **Power**

What power does grace (the law on the inside) have that the law on the outside is missing?

_____

_____

Can a person who is born again into the new kingdom still live as though the law were on the outside?

_____

_____

Lawless Living Is Graceful Living

The letter of the law is on the outside. The life and power of the Living Law is on the inside. Moses brought the law. Jesus brought grace and truth. Jesus filled in the outline of the law. Jesus fleshed out the bones of the law. Jesus took the black and white of the law and made it high-definition Technicolor. He did not change the moral law, He filled it full.

Your salvation is full-spectrum salvation. It doesn't only save you from hell, it saves you from sin. Jesus died to get you into heaven. But He lives to get heaven into you. Your full-spectrum salvation has two layers: (1) What Christ did for you—dying in your place on the Cross as an offering for your sin; and (2) Who Christ is in you—the Living Law imparting His own life and power to you now.

To secure your salvation, He fulfilled the demands of the law, which required payment for sin. *"For the wages of sin is death"* (Romans 6:23). When sin pays you what you've earned, you get death. Jesus took upon Himself what you and I have earned and deserve.

To complete your salvation, He housed Himself in you—took up residence in you—so that *"the righteous requirements of the law might be fully met* in us, *who live not according to the sinful nature but according to the Spirit"* (Romans 8:4).

I am the true Vine.—He who speaks is God, in His infinite power able to enter into us. He is man, one with us. He is the crucified One, who won a perfect righteousness and a divine life for us through His death. He is the glorified One, who from the throne gives His Spirit to make His presence real and true. He speaks—oh, listen, not to His words only, but to Himself, as He whispers secretly day by day: "I am the true Vine! All that the Vine can ever be to its branch, *I will be to you."*

Holy Lord Jesus, the heavenly Vine of God's own planting, I beseech Thee, reveal Thyself to my soul. Let the Holy Spirit, not only in thought, but in experience, give me to know all that Thou, the Son of God, art to me as the true Vine.
—Andrew Murray, *The True Vine*

When the Living Law is inside you, the law outside you is not even necessary. You can live lawlessly if you live gracefully.

DAY 5
THE POWER TO WILL AND TO DO

"It is God who works in you to will and to act according to his good purpose" (Philippians 2:13). Are you getting a glimpse of how powerful the Living Law in you can be? The law on the outside can make some progress in changing your behavior, but the law on the inside can change your heart. He can impart life and power. Can cleanse and transform.

Let's examine together 2 Corinthians 3:4–18.

Such confidence as this is ours through Christ before God. Not that we are competent in ourselves to claim anything for ourselves, but our competence comes from God. He has made us competent as ministers of a new covenant—not of the letter but of the Spirit; for the letter kills, but the Spirit gives life.
—2 Corinthians 3:4–6

_____

_____

Paul is explaining what gives his ministry its authority. Where does Paul claim that his competence originates?

_____

_____

What is Paul a minister of?

_____

_____

_____

WEEK ONE

What does Paul mean when he refers to "the letter"?

_____

_____

If Paul directly contrasts as opposites "the letter" and "the Spirit," what is he saying about the power of the law outside contrasted with the law inside?

_____

_____

Now if the ministry that brought death, which was engraved in letters on stone, came with glory, so that the Israelites could not look steadily at the face of Moses because of its glory, fading though it was, will not the ministry of the Spirit be even more glorious? If the ministry that condemns men is glorious, how much more glorious is the ministry that brings righteousness! For what was glorious has no glory now in comparison with the surpassing glory. And if what was fading away came with glory, how much greater is the glory of that which lasts!
—2 Corinthians 3:7–11

Define this phrase: *"the ministry that brought death, which was engraved in letters on stone."*

_____

_____

Why does Paul refer to the Old Covenant and the law as bringing death?

_____

_____

Did the law of the Old Covenant come with glory (the manifestation of God's presence)? How intense was the glory that accompanied the Old Covenant law? (Read Exodus 34:29–35 for context.)

_____

_____

The glory of the Old Covenant was so radiant that Moses had to cover his face with a veil, even though it was a radiance that faded away between Moses's encounters with God. It was not a permanent radiance. The skin of Moses's face reflected the presence of God—a radiance that came from the outside and faded away progressively. I'll summarize Paul this way: "The law came with stunning glory—the presence of God so near that the skin on Moses's face was transformed by it. The Old Covenant law came with a glory that had never been seen before. The glory of the Old Covenant is nothing to dismiss."

Summarize what Paul is saying in the rest of the statement from verses 7–11. In comparison to the New Covenant law, how does the Old stack up?

_____

_____

_____

Therefore, since we have such a hope, we are very bold. We are not like Moses, who would put a veil over his face to keep the Israelites from gazing at it while the radiance was fading away.
—2 Corinthians 3:12–13

We are not like Moses, who put a veil over his face to hide the glory that was fading. Paul is not suggesting that Moses hid the glory on his face because it was fading. He is suggesting that the glory on Moses's face, though outward and temporary—*even that glory* was so spectacular that the people could not gaze on it. He has already made the point that the glory of our covenant so far surpasses the glory that transformed Moses's appearance that the Old Covenant glory seems like nothing in comparison.

Set Apart

The glory of God is His presence in a manifested form. The glory of God in the Old Covenant transformed Moses's outward appearance, but the glory of God in the New Covenant transforms our hearts. It is not a glory fading away, but it instead is growing brighter. We do not have to hide it under a veil.

Summarize what Paul is saying in verses 12–13.

_____

_____

_____

_____

But their minds were made dull, for to this day the same veil remains when the old covenant is read. It has not been removed, because only in Christ is it taken away. Even to this day when Moses is read, a veil covers their hearts. But whenever anyone turns to the Lord, the veil is taken away.
—2 Corinthians 3:14–16

Paul continues his explanation. What was the outcome in the lives of those who did not look fully on the glory of God, but instead knew His glory secondhand?

_____

_____

The physical veil that hid the glory on Moses's face has now become a spiritual veil. Describe that veil and what it hides.

_____

_____

How is that veil removed?

_____

_____

_____

Now the Lord is the Spirit, and where the Spirit of the Lord is, there is freedom. And we, who with unveiled faces all reflect the Lord's glory, are being transformed into his likeness with ever-increasing glory, which comes from the Lord, who is the Spirit.
—2 Corinthians 3:17–18

Whenever anyone turns to the Lord, the veil is taken away, Paul tell us. How does he then identify "the Lord"?
"The Lord is _____."

"Where the Spirit of the Lord is, there is _____."

In the New Covenant law, where is the Spirit of the Lord?

_____

_____

What does the law on the inside give you?

_____

_____

What does the law on the inside free you from?

_____

_____

In the New Covenant who reflects the Lord's glory?

_____

_____

What is the difference between the Lord's glory on the inside and the Lord's glory on the outside?

_____

_____

_____

Moses's glory was fading away. What is our glory doing?

_____

_____

❦ ❦ ❦

Ever-Increasing Glory

"We...are being transformed into his likeness with ever-increasing glory" (2 Corinthians 3:18).

Moses was changed on the outside and that change faded. We are transformed on the inside, and that inner transformation gets reflected on the outside. Moses did not need a veil for himself when he spoke intimately with God. *"The LORD would speak to Moses face to face, as a man speaks with his friend"* (Exodus 33:11). The veil on Moses's face was only for the people We, like Moses, have unveiled faces. Our contact with God is face-to-face. Moses, for whom God was still outside, hints at our direct access to the presence of God when the Lord is on the inside. Unveiled.

Our inner transformation becomes more and more evident. Instead of fading away, the presence of God is reflected more vividly. Ever-increasing glory.

Insider Trading

When the law moves to the inside, embodied in Jesus, the Living Law, you trade your efforts for His power. You trade your weakness for His strength. You trade your inability for His ability.

Nothing in the New Covenant ever, ever tells you to renew yourself. It tells you to *"be renewed"* (Ephesians 4:23, NASB). The verb tense means that you are acted upon. Give up the power of you, and live in the power of Him. You can't do both. Trade one in for the other.

The New Covenant is all about Christ in you. The Old Covenant was the proving ground. It demonstrated that no power outside you will transform you. Scripture hammers home this truth, repeating it in words and pictures from beginning to end.

Scripture's Kaleidoscope

God has filled His Word with pictures of the transforming power of Christ in you. The active evidence of grace is writ large. Let's look through the kaleidoscope and view the patterns that converge to reveal the beautiful reality of the power of grace.

In 2 Corinthians 3:3–18, which you examined in detail yesterday, what was the focus of God's work? *"Being transformed into his likeness."* In Romans 8:29 we also read that we are being *"conformed to the likeness of his Son."* Let's examine how this conforming and transforming is being accomplished.

We are being transformed into His likeness by His life in us. The law on the inside. Grace. We are only the containers for His power.

We've already looked at the example of Jesus as the true Vine. In *He Restores My Soul,* I used a similar glove-and-hand analogy, borrowed from Major W. Ian Thomas's *The Saving Life of Christ.* Major Thomas makes the point that a glove's only purpose is to be filled with a hand. Then, everything that is possible to the hand has become possible to the glove. To further illustrate Jesus's point, I wrote:

> The glove has no life in itself, but it was created to contain and express life. *When I fill a glove with the life of my hand, the glove is transformed into the image of my hand.* Everything my hand does, it does through the glove, but the focus is my hand, not the glove. If I were to shake your hand while wearing my glove, you would not say, "I shook Jennifer Dean's glove." You would say, "I shook Jennifer Dean's hand." Whatever comes into contact with my glove has come into contact with my hand. My hand expresses itself through the glove....
>
> You could reason, "Apart from the hand the glove can do nothing"; but "the glove can do all things through the hand that gives it strength." Furthermore, "He has given the glove life, and this life is in the hand. The glove that has the hand has life; the glove that does not have

WEEK ONE

the hand does not have life" (paraphrase of John 15:5; Philippians 4:13; 1 John 5:11–12).

In another example, consider the words of Jesus from John 7:37–39.

> On the last and greatest day of the Feast, Jesus stood and said in a loud voice, "If anyone is thirsty, let him come to me and drink. Whoever believes in me, as the Scripture has said, streams of living water will flow from within him." By this he meant the Spirit, whom those who believed in him were later to receive.

Living water that flows in becomes living water than flows out.

Imagine a clear glass. Imagine that glass filled with dirty, nasty, contaminated water. Scum floating on the top. Debris sitting on the bottom. Unidentified particles of stuff throughout. Do you see it?

Now, take that glass and turn it upside down and empty it. Is the glass clean? If you pour more water in, will the new water be clean? The water will pick up the grunge left on the inside of the glass and immediately become dirty water.

Now, see the glass of dirty water again in your mind's eye. This time, take the glass of dirty water and put it under a faucet flowing with fresh water. Let the water flow into the glass. Do you see what happens? The flow of fresh water displaces the dirty water. It disrupts the sediment on the bottom. It progressively changes the inside of the glass until it is clean and the water it is holding is clean and the water splashing over the edges and flowing out around it is clean.

The secret is the continual fresh flow of clean water on the inside. The life of Christ flowing freely in you, flowing freely from you. Clean—first inside, then outside. (For more word-picture examples from the Word, see *He Restores My Soul*.)

The Shape of Grace

In King Jesus's inaugural address, the Sermon on the Mount, He laid out how grace looks in our lives. He described and defined the heart of the law. He would then live out loud everything He proclaimed, demonstrating grace in action. This study will examine the heart that will produce the actions consistent with Christ's likeness.

Recall that when Moses gave the Ten Commandments, the people found it impossible to obey them. Under grace, we will discover that which once came as command, now comes as promise. Everything God requires of you, He provides for you. Everything that He laid out in the Ten Commandments is a promise of what He will accomplish in you. Rather than being impossible to obey, the law will become our natural inclination.

Beware of placing our Lord as Teacher first instead of Savior. That tendency is prevalent today, and it is a dangerous tendency. We must know Him first as Savior before His teaching can have any meaning for us or before it can have any meaning other than that of an ideal that leads to despair. Fancy coming to men and women with defective lives and defiled hearts and wrong mainsprings, and telling them to be pure in heart! What is the use of giving us an ideal we cannot possibly attain? We are happier without it. If Jesus is a teacher only, then all He can do is to tantalize us by erecting a standard we cannot come anywhere near. Bit if by being born again from above we know Him first as Savior, we know that He did not come to teach us only. He came to make us what He teaches we should be. The Sermon on the Mount is a statement of the life we will live when the Holy Spirit is having His way with us.
—Oswald Chambers, *Studies in the Sermon on the Mount*

We are able to live in the state of blessedness that God has created for us when we discover the key to true holiness. Rather than an uphill climb or a crushing burden, the call to holiness is a call to freedom and joy. We were made for holiness, and holiness is the best fit for our lives. We have been set apart by God, and we are grace-shaped. Only holiness fits us.

The promise is not happiness, but blessedness. Happiness is transitory and driven by circumstance while blessedness is eternal and grounded in the reality of Christ in you. Blessedness leads to true happiness because, when viewed through the eternal grid, circumstances lose their power to toss your emotions around "like a wave driven by the wind."

Consider the following statements and highlight the wording that indicates the location of the power of God. Where is the epicenter of God's power located?

To this end I labor, struggling with all his energy, which so power-fully works in me.
—Colossians 1:29

Now to him who is able to do immeasurably more than all we ask or imagine, according to his power that is at work within us.
—Ephesians 3:20

WEEK TWO

DAY 1

THE BLESSEDS

Today we begin to look more closely at the Sermon on the Mount, carefully studying the Beatitudes as the foundation upon which Jesus would build this discourse and live His earthly life.

Jesus introduced His inaugural address, His state of the kingdom speech, with a series of statements that were framed in a vocabulary familiar to His audience. "Blessed are...." In last week's study I provided a deeper context for our understanding of the word *blessed*. It means a state in which you can continually live because of the life of Christ in you, the law on the inside. It is not a reward for a behavior but a condition of the heart. Thus, in the sentence structure of the Beatitudes, *"Blessed are the poor in spirit"* means that when you are poor in spirit, the natural state of your soul is blessedness. The outcome of being poor in spirit is a state of blessedness. It is a description instead of a command. It is the promise He is making about that which He will provide, and it is the description of the heart from which holy living flows. It describes a life set apart.

Jesus is saying that blessedness is the natural and inescapable outcome of certain conditions—being poor in spirit for example. In his study, *The Beatitudes,* Spiros Zodhiates explains it this way:

> It is similar to a doctor's saying, "If you rest, if you take this medicine, the result will be thus and so." That is what the Lord does here. He says that where the condition of poverty of spirit exists, the result is blessedness. This is the pronouncement of One who knows. He diagnoses, He prescribes, and He foretells the result.

Read through the following examples stated in the same form as the Beatitudes. These are just a very few of the many, many statements found in the Bible with this format. From the context, see if the understanding of *blessed* I have proposed fits. Summarize each passage in your words, paying attention to the Hebrew concept of "blessed."

Blessed is the man
who does not walk in the counsel of the wicked
or stand in the way of sinners
or sit in the seat of mockers.
—Psalm 1:1

_____

_____

_____

Blessed is he whose transgressions are forgiven,
whose sins are covered.
Blessed is the man whose sin the LORD does not count against him
and in whose spirit is no deceit.
—Psalm 32:1–2

Blessed are those whose strength is in you,
    who have set their hearts on pilgrimage.
—**Psalm 84:5**

Blessed are those who have learned to acclaim you,
    who walk in the light of your presence, O LORD.
—**Psalm 89:15**

Blessed Are the Poor in Spirit

His ministry had just started. Publicly launched at His recent baptism by John the Baptist and anchored during His 40 days and nights in the desert, which concluded in a show-down with His enemy, Jesus was like the new kid on the block. The word was out that there was a new rabbi on the scene. He had been preaching and teaching and healing, and was drawing larger crowds each day.

"Now when he saw the crowds, he went up on a mountainside and sat down. His disciples came to him, and he began to teach them" (Matthew 5:1–2). He gathered His newly named, inner-circle disciples close, and the crowds who wanted to listen stood or sat behind them. Rabbi Jesus, in typical rabbinical style, sat down—a sign that He was about to expound the Scriptures.

Day 1: The Blesseds

The mountainside made it easier for Him to speak to the eager, curious crowd. It made for good acoustics and gave everyone a good view of Him. It afforded something like a stadium setting.

Here He is, the new rabbi. The subject of all the buzz. This was apparently His first big gathering and His first substantive address, though He had been teaching in their synagogues. What would He say? How would He use His new notoriety? What agenda would He push? Would He razzle-dazzle them? Would He scold and rant?

His first words were these: *"Blessed are the poor in spirit, for theirs is the kingdom of heaven"* (Matthew 5:3).

The Greek word that is translated as "poor" is a word that implies being destitute, with no ability to provide for themselves, completely dependent on others to supply their needs. A beggar. He could have used a less stark word that would mean the working poor, those who just got by day to day. Instead, He used a word that meant utterly, abjectly impoverished.

The very first thing He wanted to say about the new kingdom was that it belonged to those who recognized that they were incapable of providing spiritually for themselves. They brought nothing with them that would gain them entrance to the kingdom. They could do nothing that would give them stature in the kingdom. They could only possess the kingdom by receiving all from the hand of another.

This is the foundational law for how the kingdom works. Everything else will build on this. Being poor in spirit is not just the way into the kingdom, but it is the way of life in the kingdom. This is the fundamental reality of the kingdom. "Nothing in my hand I bring/simply to the cross I cling" (from the hymn, *Rock of Ages*). This is how we enter in the first place, and how we operate in the kingdom every minute.

Consider the imagery in these statements about the kingdom. Write out the implications of Jesus's words.

"Let the little children come to me, and do not hinder them, for the kingdom of God belongs to such as these. I tell you the truth, anyone who will not receive the kingdom of God like a little child will never enter it."
—Mark 10:14–15

Set Apart

_____

_____

"I tell you the truth, no one can see the kingdom of God unless he is born again."
—John 3:3

_____

_____

_____

❧ ❧ ❧

A little child does not feel obligated nor is able to provide his own living, or shelter, or provision. A little child takes it as the natural state of things that someone will provide for her. A newborn baby is an more dramatic image. Capable of offering nothing. Able only to receive what is offered. Helpless, weak, poor.

Celebrating Weakness, Prizing Emptiness

"Oh! That's too easy!" some will say. I suggest the opposite. Nothing is harder for our flesh than to come empty-handed, needy, and weak. To be stripped bare, emptied out, impotent, exposed—it is the secret fear we all harbor. It is the stuff of nightmares and anxiety attacks. And it is the kingdom's requirement for citizenship.

> *I will boast all the more gladly about my weaknesses, so that Christ's power may rest on me. That is why, for Christ's sake, I delight in weaknesses, in insults, in hardships, in persecutions, in difficulties. For when I am weak, then I am strong.*
> —2 Corinthians 12:9–10

My weakness is my greatest asset in the kingdom. My weakness is where God meets me. My weakness is where Christ's power is most clearly displayed in me. Only when I am confronted with my own helplessness can I experience the power of Christ in me.

Your helplessness is your best prayer. It calls from your heart to the heart of God with greater effect than all your uttered pleas. He hears it from the very moment that you are seized with helplessness, and He becomes actively engaged at once in hearing and answering the prayer of your helplessness.

—O. Hallesby, *Prayer*

I recently had the tiniest glimpse of how powerfully helplessness speaks. A few years ago, I lost my husband to brain cancer. During the final months of his illness, he became utterly helpless. The man I had leaned on for 25 years, whose strength I counted on, was now dependent upon me for his every need. During those weeks, my ear was tuned to his every sigh, his every restless movement, every change in his breathing pattern. If I had to be out of his room for even a few minutes, I had a monitor with me so I could hear him if he needed me. When he was strong, I was not so attentive. His needs did not fill my waking moments, when he could meet them himself. His helplessness spoke louder than any word he might have spoken. Because of his helplessness—because I knew he could do nothing on his own—I was on watch day and night.

My experience is but a pale shadow of the reality of the kingdom, but still it helps me understand how my weakness is the opening for His strength. The fact of my helplessness is the only prayer I need. It speaks louder than eloquence.

We are all helpless when it comes to things spiritual. We may not have recognized it yet, but we are all destitute and wholly dependent on Jesus for any hint of goodness, or any true remorse that would result in repentance, or any wisdom or knowledge of the kingdom. We have nothing to offer. We can all agree with Paul's conclusion: *"I know that nothing good lives in me, that is, in my sinful nature"* (Romans 7:18). We are all helpless, but until we recognize it and accept it, we will not know the blessedness of helplessness. Jesus said, *"It is not the healthy who need a doctor, but the sick. But go and learn what this means: 'I desire mercy, not sacrifice.' For I have not come to call the righteous, but sinners"* (Matthew 9:12–13).

Let your helplessness and your weakness be the offering you bring to Him. He is not waiting for you to be strong. He is waiting for you to recognize that you are weak.

What if the branch said, "I wonder what I could give to the vine?" What if the glove said, "I wonder how I could be worthy of the hand?" Do you see what silliness that would be? The vine wants nothing from the branch except to be the container of its life. The hand wants nothing of the glove except for the glove to rest on the hand.

Set Apart

**Spend some time right now admitting and embracing your helpless-
ness and your weakness. Spend time in the Father's presence. Come
to Him as a little child. Don't try to be anything except what you
truly are—poor in spirit. Journal your thoughts here.**

_____

_____

_____

_____

_____

_____

❧ ❧ ❧

WEEK TWO

DAY 2

EMPTY

"May the God of hope fill you with all joy and peace as you trust in him, so that you may overflow with hope by the power of the Holy Spirit" (Romans 15:13). To be filled, we must be emptied. The person who admits that she is destitute in spirit is willing to empty herself of everything that she once trusted or anything that she ever prized because she thought it made her valuable. God wants you full of the joy and peace found only in Jesus. Anything other than Jesus just gets in His way.

"We have this treasure in jars of clay to show that this all-surpassing power is from God and not from us" (2 Corinthians 4:7). When the Scripture talks about clay or clay jars, it usually symbolizes human beings. God wants to fill you up with His great treasure. And what is the content of His great treasure? *"[N]amely, Christ, in whom are hidden all the treasures of wisdom and knowledge"* (Colossians 2:2–3). Filled with Christ. Christ in you. The law on the inside.

I wrote in *He Restores My Soul*:

You and I are clay jars into which the Father has poured His presence, His power, His Spirit. What is the requirement for a clay jar? What does the Father need from you to fill you with Himself? He needs your emptiness.

Read the following passage and answer the questions.

The wife of a man from the company of the prophets cried out to Elisha, "Your servant my husband is dead, and you know that he revered the Lord. But now his creditor is coming to take my two boys as his slaves."

Elisha replied to her, "How can I help you? Tell me, what do you have in your house?"

"Your servant has nothing there at all," she said, "except a little oil."

Elisha said, "Go around and ask all your neighbors for empty jars. Don't ask for just a few. Then go inside and shut the door behind you and your sons. Pour oil into all the jars, and as each is filled, put it to one side."

She left him and afterward shut the door behind her and her sons. They brought the jars to her and she kept pouring. When all the jars were full, she said to her son, "Bring me another one."

But he replied, "There is not a jar left." Then the oil stopped flowing.

—2 Kings 4:1–6

Do you see how the widow represents the poor in spirit? What was her situation?

_____

_____

When Elisha asked her what she possessed, what was her reply?

_____

Did she have anything with which to meet her own needs? Did she have any source of supply?

_____

Would you agree that her cry to Elisha was a confession of her help-lessness?

_____

She had *"a little oil."* Oil is most often a symbol of the Spirit. The story is a true account, but also has layers of spiritual meaning, as does all Scripture. In the symbolism of the story, I think the fact that she had a little oil means that she had entered the kingdom. Now let's observe how fullness in the kingdom comes out of empti-ness. She is poverty stricken. She is dependent upon a supply that must come from another hand.

Why did Elisha help her? Why did her neighbors help her? Because she acknowledged what?

_____

What kind of jars did Elisha tell her to ask for?

_____

_____

How many jars—how much emptiness—did she need?

_____

_____

When the oil began to flow into her emptiness, what did _"a little oil"_ **become?**

_____

_____

_____

When did the oil stop flowing?

_____

_____

In the kingdom, it is a great advantage to be poor in spirit. The more emptiness you bring to the Lord, the more filling you will receive. Acknowledging our emptiness starts the filling. And the Oil flows in the kingdom until every last corner of emptiness is filled to overflowing. Blessed are the poor in spirit.

Like-Minded

The Beatitudes describe the inner life of Jesus, and the Sermon on the Mount is His promise that He will express His life through you. If Jesus holds up being poor in spirit as a mark of holiness and a life set apart, then Jesus must be poor in spirit. I know. It is disconcerting to think so. But, He is poor in spirit by choice.

Set Apart

He is not—and was not while on earth—poor in spirit by nature. It makes it all the more astounding that He, who could have clutched tightly His rightful position in heaven, instead voluntarily let it go. Paul describes it this way:

> *Your attitude should be the same as that of Christ Jesus:*
>   *Who, being in very nature God,*
>   *did not consider equality with God something to be grasped,*
>   *but made himself nothing,*
>   *taking the very nature of a servant,*
>   *being made in human likeness.*
>   *And being found in appearance as a man,*
>   *he humbled himself*
>   *and became obedient to death—*
>   *even death on a cross!*
>   *Therefore God exalted him to the highest place*
>   *and gave him the name that is above every name,*
>   *that at the name of Jesus every knee should bow,*
>   *in heaven and on earth and under the earth,*
>   *and every tongue confess that Jesus Christ is Lord,*
>   *to the glory of God the Father.*
> —Philippians 2:5–11

Jesus—King of kings, Creator of all that exists, Sustainer of all creation, In-the-Beginning God—made Himself nothing, took the very nature of a servant, humbled Himself, became obedient. Put Himself under the authority of the Father. All by choice. And the outcome? His is the kingdom. *"The kingdom of the world has become the kingdom of our Lord and of his Christ, and he will reign forever and ever"* (Revelation 11:15).

Consider the fact that Jesus left the universe's throne and humbled Himself and took the role of a servant, serving those whom He had Himself created. In *Pursuing the Christ*, I reflect on this holy moment:

What must that moment have been like? When heaven's great Treasure shed His kingly grandeur and donned mere clay, did the angels for a moment hold their breath and look on in astonishment? When He who was from the beginning took upon Himself the form of a servant, did the eternal realm halt—just for a heartbeat—and stand speechless with wonder? When the King of kings exchanged His majestic robes for swaddling clothes, surely it was the most beautiful, awe-inspiring moment in all eternity.

On earth, it was a little-noticed event. A young peasant couple and a few poor shepherds were the only witnesses to an ordinary birth in an ordinary place at an ordinary time. No pomp or ceremony. No grand announcement to a waiting crowd. No dancing in the streets.

In the heavens, that which looked ordinary from the earth was the spark for unparalleled celebration (Hebrews 1:6). It was something never before seen and never to be seen again—when the King became a servant.

This is the heart that Jesus is producing in you. Here is how Paul said such a heart looks in action: *"Do nothing out of selfish ambition or vain conceit, but in humility consider others better than yourselves. Each of you should look not only to your own interests, but also to the interests of others"* (Philippians 2:3–4). These are the words that introduce Paul's description of Jesus's humility, voluntarily making Himself poor in spirit (vv. 5–11).

Ponder the stunning portrait of Jesus's heart in Philippians 2:3–11. Soak it in, linger on each phrase until it burrows into your heart. Amazing grace.

What circumstances or relationships or challenges are you dealing with right now that call for the inconceivable humility that only Jesus can impart to you?

_____

_____

_____

_____

Would you admit right now that such condescension is not possible for you. Your flesh fights it at every turn. But in this moment, you can choose to empty yourself of pride and rigidity and receive the fullness of Jesus, whose love compelled Him to humble Himself and become a servant. Write out your thoughts.

_____

_____

_____

_____

_____

🝔 🝔 🝔

DAY 3

THE FATHER SUPPLIES ALL

"I tell you the truth, the Son can do nothing by himself; he can do only what he sees his Father doing, because whatever the Father does the Son also does. For the Father loves the Son and shows him all he does."
—John 5:19–20

The Son can do nothing by Himself. Jesus receives all from the Father. While on earth in the form of a servant, Jesus was the glove and the Father was the hand.

"When you lift up the Son of Man, then you will know that I am He, and I do nothing on My own initiative, but I speak these things as the Father taught me" (John 8:28 NASB). The Father expressed Himself through Jesus. Jesus *"made himself nothing"* so that the Father would be on display.

In the following statements of Jesus, highlight words and phrases that indicate He was poor in spirit—that He was willing to depend on the Father for everything.

"If I glorify Myself, My glory is nothing. It is My Father who glorifies Me."
—John 8:54 (NASB)

"For I did not speak on My own initiative, but the Father Himself who sent Me has given Me a commandment as to what to say and what to speak. I know that His commandment is eternal life; therefore the things I speak just as the Father has told Me."
—John 12:49–50 (NASB)

"Don't you believe that I am in the Father, and that the Father is in me? The words I say to you are not just my own. Rather, it is the Father, living in me, who is doing his work."
—John 14:10

"These words you hear are not my own; they belong to the Father who sent me."
—John 14:24

"The world must learn that I love the Father and that I do exactly what my Father has commanded me."
—**John 14:31**

Like Father, Like Son

In the same way that Jesus related to the Father while on earth, we are now to relate to Jesus.

Jesus's Relationship to the Father	Your Relationship to Jesus
The Son can do nothing by himself (John 5:19).	*Apart from me, you can do nothing* (John 15:5).
The Father…shows him all he does (John 5:20).	*I too will…show myself to him* (John 14:21). *Everything that I have learned from my Father, I have made known to you* (John 15:15).
I am in the Father, and…the Father is in me (John 14:10).	*If a man remains in me and I in him* (John 15:5).
The Son may bring glory to the Father (John 14:13).	*Glory has come to me through them* (John 17:10).
The Father knows me and I know the Father (John 10:15).	*I know my sheep and my sheep know me* (John 10:14).

The more willing we are to humble ourselves and confess that we are poor in spirit and destitute except for the provision of Christ in us, the more we will experience the life of Christ. Blessed are the poor in spirit.

Bringing Nothing, Gaining Everything

When you become a citizen of the kingdom, you fully give yourself to the King. The kingdom is more than just those parts of your life that you consider "spiritual" or "religious." The King will supply all your needs. He knows your physical and financial needs as well as He knows your spiritual and emotional needs. He takes responsibility for all of your life as He creates holiness in you. When the King counts His treasure, He counts you. *"They will be mine," says the Lord Almighty, "in the day when I make up my treasured possession"* (Malachi 3:17). Did you get that? You are His treasured possession. He has set you apart. He takes care of you, guards you, protects you. Everything He has, He uses on your behalf. It's a pretty good trade. You give Him your nothing, and He gives you His everything.

Jesus, in His inaugural address, added some detail to explain what it is like to be utterly dependent and abjectly poor when you are in the kingdom.

"For this reason I say to you, do not be worried about your life, as to what you will eat or what you will drink; nor for your body, as to what you will put on. Is not life more than food, and the body more than clothing? Look at the birds of the air, that they do not sow, nor reap nor gather into barns, and yet your heavenly Father feeds them. Are you not worth much more than they? And who of you by being worried can add a single hour to his life?

"And why are you worried about clothing? Observe how the lilies of the field grow; they do not toil nor do they spin, yet I say to you that not even Solomon in all his glory clothed himself like one of these. But if God so clothes the grass of the field, which is alive today and tomorrow is thrown into the furnace, will He not much more clothe you? You of little faith! Do not worry then, saying, 'What will we eat?' or 'What will we drink?' or 'What will we wear for clothing?' For the Gentiles eagerly seek all these things; for your heavenly Father knows that you need all these things. But seek first His kingdom and His righteousness, and all these things will be added to you. So do not worry about tomorrow; for tomorrow will care for itself. Each day has enough trouble of its own."
—Matthew 6:25–34

Using Matthew 6:25–34 as your reference point, consider these questions:

Set Apart

Does Jesus promise you that even your physical and material needs are met out of heaven's abundance?

_____

Since worrying does not accomplish anything, how can you transform worrying into trusting?

_____

_____

Highlight the phrase that assures you that your Father is aware of your physical needs. Let the certainty of that settle on you.

_____

_____

Write out what this sentence is saying to you right now in your present circumstances: _"But seek first his kingdom and his righteousness, and all these things will be given to you as well."_

_____

_____

_____

❧ ❧ ❧

The Father created you so that you have physical and material needs, as well as spiritual and emotional needs. He wants you to depend on Him for every part of your life.

For Theirs Is the Kingdom

When the type of phrasing Jesus used in the Beatitudes appears in Scripture, it usually includes a clarification about what "blessed" will look like for such a person.

In the following Scriptures, identify the description of blessedness.

Blessed is the man who does not walk in the counsel of the wicked
*   or stand in the way of sinners or sit in the seat of mockers.*
But his delight is in the law of the Lord,
*   and on his law he meditates day and night.*
He is like a tree planted by streams of water,
*   which yields its fruit in season*
*   and whose leaf does not wither.*
Whatever he does prospers.
—Psalm 1:1–3

Blessed is he who has regard for the weak;
*   the Lord delivers him in times of trouble.*
The Lord will protect him and preserve his life;
*   he will bless him in the land*
*   and not surrender him to the desire of his foes.*
The Lord will sustain him on his sickbed
*   and restore him from his bed of illness.*
—Psalm 41:1–3

Blessed are those you choose
*   and bring near to live in your courts!*
We are filled with the good things of your house,
*   of your holy temple.*
—Psalm 65:4

You can see that Jesus is teaching in familiar patterns and that the form of His statements was according to tradition. The content of His teaching was explosive, but it came in a recognized cadence.

"Blessed are the poor in spirit, for theirs is the kingdom of heaven." The poor in spirit—those who recognize their complete dependence upon the King for everything—live in a state of blessedness and that blessedness is characterized by this: theirs is the kingdom of heaven.

Jesus's message was that the kingdom had already arrived and was there for the taking. When the Word became flesh, the kingdom of heaven invaded earth. Jesus sometimes talked of the kingdom in future terms, when at the end of the age the kingdom would be physically established. But He primarily talked of the present form the kingdom takes.

His kingdom is not of this world, He said. His kingdom is present on the earth, but it is another dimension of reality.

Once, having been asked by the Pharisees when the kingdom of God would come, Jesus replied, *"The kingdom of God does not come with your careful observation, nor will people say, 'Here it is,' or 'There it is,' because the kingdom of God is within you"* (Luke 17:20–21). In the Old Testament, the kingdom of God was represented by the land of Canaan. The Promised Land. He described the Promised Land as a land of rest. Canaan was the set apart land for the set apart people.

Understanding the land of Canaan to be a foreshadowing of the kingdom of heaven, what do you see in these descriptions of the Promised Land that give you insight into the kingdom? Write out your thoughts.

You are not to do as we do here today, everyone as he sees fit, since you have not yet reached **the resting place** *and the inheritance the* LORD *your God is giving you. But you will cross the Jordan and settle in the land the* LORD *your God is giving you as an inheritance, and he will give you rest from all your enemies around you so that you will live in safety.*
—Deuteronomy 12:8–11 (author's emphasis)

"Praise be to the LORD, *who has given rest to his people Israel just as he promised. Not one word has failed of all the good promises he gave through his servant Moses. May the* LORD *our God be with us as he was with our fathers; may he never leave us nor forsake us. May he turn our hearts to him, to walk in all his ways and to keep the commands, decrees and regulations he gave our fathers. And may*

these words of mine, which I have prayed before the LORD, be near to the LORD our God day and night, that he may uphold the cause of his servant and the cause of his people Israel according to each day's need, so that all the peoples of the earth may know that the LORD is God and that there is no other. But your hearts must be fully committed to the LORD our God, to live by his decrees and obey his commands, as at this time."
—1 Kings 8:56–61 (author's emphasis)

———————————————————————

———————————————————————

———————————————————————

———————————————————————

Those who are poor in spirit are living out the experience of the present kingdom of heaven in their lives. They are being transformed into the likeness of the King, moment by moment. They are being supplied by the riches of heaven and cared for as is fitting the King's treasured ones. They can live with their souls at rest.

Blessed are the poor in spirit, for theirs is the kingdom of heaven.

DAY 4

BLESSED ARE THOSE WHO MOURN

Life on planet earth is punctuated with mourning. A promise of escape from sorrow does not take effect until we escape our physical, earth-bound bodies. Our eternal home is free of sorrow, but this earth is not.

Jesus once said to His disciples, *"I have told you these things, so that in me you may have peace. In this world you will have trouble. But take heart! I have overcome the world"* (John 16:33). He promised them trouble and sorrow while in the world, but at the same time, peace and overcoming in Him. Living in the world, yet dwelling in the kingdom.

The promise of the kingdom is not that you will be spared sorrow or disappointment or heartache, but rather that any difficulty that comes into your life will have good as its goal. Paul evaluated his situation this way: *"For our light and momentary troubles are achieving for us an eternal glory that far outweighs them all. So we fix our eyes not on what is seen, but on what is unseen. For what is seen is temporary, but what is unseen is eternal"* (2 Corinthians 4:17–18).

Whatever produces mourning in your life, you can describe it with Paul's words: *"light and momentary troubles."* Oh, I know it doesn't feel light and momentary. I know that many times it feels crushing and overwhelming and unbearable. It seems that this mourning will have no end.

Perspective is everything. You are now living in the eternal kingdom. Earth and time are not the template for your circumstances. Whatever you are experiencing right now, the glory it is producing outweighs the pain it is causing. It is producing an eternal weight of glory.

If your perspective is confined to the now, then your circumstances may overwhelm you. If you do as Paul suggests—fix your eyes on what is unseen and eternal rather than what is seen and temporal—you will discover that the King rules the kingdom and He is in charge of anything and everything in your life. If the call to holiness has not found a response in your heart, then nothing will give you comfort. But if you have allowed the reality of your kingdom citizenship to fill your horizon, then even in calamity and heartache, you will have comfort, hope, and joy. Even in disastrous upheaval, you will live in a state of blessedness. Even occasions for mourning can be received with rejoicing.

God's children run home when the storm comes on. It is the heaven-born instinct of a gracious soul to seek shelter from all ills beneath the wings of Jehovah.
—C. H. Spurgeon, *Evening by Evening*

Difficulty and pain drive us to the heart of God, where blessed comfort is found.

Look at Paul's words and think through the questions.

Therefore, since we have been justified through faith, we have peace with God through our Lord Jesus Christ, through whom we have gained access by faith into this grace in which we now stand. And we rejoice in the hope of the glory of God. Not only so, but we also rejoice in our sufferings, because we know that suffering produces perseverance; perseverance, character; and character, hope. And hope does not disappoint us, because God has poured out his love into our hearts by the Holy Spirit, whom he has given us
—Romans 5:1–5

In verses 1 and 2, Paul defines the background against which everything else will be viewed. What is the context of Paul's assertion about suffering?

_____

_____

Why does Paul say that he rejoices in suffering? What will suffering produce that outweighs its pain?

_____

What does Paul say he hopes for? *"And we rejoice in the hope* ____
_____.***"***

Paul concludes that hope does not disappoint us. When we get what we hoped we would get, then hope has not disappointed us. Again, what did Paul hope for in his suffering?

_____

_____

And what did Paul's suffering produce that caused him to say that hope does not disappoint?

_____

_____

❧ ❧ ❧

Mourning Glory

The commentator William Barclay notes that the Greek word used in Matthew 5:4 gives the sense of the strongest grief (The Daily Bible Study Series). Wailing, lamenting, groaning. Ripping the garments. Sackcloth and ashes. Blessed are the overwhelmed with grief. They will be comforted.

The Scripture speaks of mourning in a variety of forms and for a plethora of reasons. Each one is the setting for the glory of God being incubated in our lives. As we are changed from one degree of glory to the next, hope does not disappoint. The hope of the glory of God is realized when we rejoice in our sufferings.

We mourn, first, over our own sins. When the reality of my sinfulness hits me, it grieves me. Especially when it suddenly strikes me that I have hurt someone, the realization pains me and causes me to groan inwardly, feeling pain until I can find the comfort of forgiveness. Yet, if I never felt any pain over my sins, I would never know the freedom of forgiveness.

"Even now," declares the LORD, "return to me with all your heart, with fasting and weeping and mourning" (Joel 2:12). I mourn over what my sins have done to others. Yet the God of all comfort reminds me that just as He has made a way for me to be forgiven, He has not neglected planning for the healing and restoration of any person my sins have hurt.

I mourn over times my sins have poisoned a relationship. And the God of all comfort reminds me that He is able even to resurrect relationships and bring the power of forgiveness to bear on the most battered heart.

I mourn over how my sin affects the heart of the Father. And the God of all comfort reminds me that He has removed my sins as far from me as the east is from the west; that He does not count my sins against me.

Have you mourned over your sins? Are you mourning over sin right now for any reason?

_____

_____

What is the comfort you receive as you repent?

_____

_____

The decorative ornaments between sections.

We mourn over the sins of others. We see the effect of sin in the lives of those we love, and we mourn and pray with great fervency. All the power of God flows from heaven to earth through the prayers of His people. Mourning over the sins of others is often what drives us to pray for them and keeps us praying for them, and so keeps them in position for the power and provision of God to invade their lives. The tremendous joy of seeing a prodigal return to the Father, or a lost sheep found by the Shepherd, is the kind of joy that sparks celebration.

> _Those who sow in tears_
> _will reap with songs of joy._
> _He who goes out weeping,_
> _carrying seed to sow,_
> _will return with songs of joy,_
> _carrying sheaves with him._
> —Psalm 126:5–6

Mourning over others' sins sets the wheels of heaven in motion so that what comes out of that mourning is beyond what you can ask or think. You might be in mourning for someone else's sin right now. The God of all comfort reassures you that your tears are watering the very ground His hand has plowed and His Spirit has planted. You are agreeing with Him and it is His heart being reproduced in you.

Sidebar text "WEEK TWO"
WEEK TWO

Is there someone in your life over whose sins you are mourning? Tell the Lord everything about it. Write out your thoughts.

_____

_____

What comfort do you receive?

_____

We mourn when sorrows come into our lives. Life on this earth has sorrow and loss and disappointment. This is a given and there is no way around it. But the God of all comfort is always present, providing peace that is beyond understanding. He redeems our mourning, using it to add a depth, richness, and texture to our lives that would otherwise be missing. Through sorrow, we learn perspective and proportion. What matters and what doesn't. Sorrow can strip us of the superfluous, leaving our hearts leaner and stronger and less encumbered. In deep grief, there is an experience of supernatural comfort that defies words. The one who never knows grief will lose out on the opportunity to know that comfort.

Isaiah proclaims what the Messiah is sent to do. He explains what the Messiah has anointing—power and authority—to accomplish.

> _The Spirit of the Sovereign L_ord _is on me,_
> _because the L_ord _has anointed me_
> _to preach good news to the poor._
> _He has sent me to bind up the brokenhearted,_
> _to proclaim freedom for the captives_
> _and release from darkness for the prisoners,_
> _to proclaim the year of the L_ord's _favor_
> _and the day of vengeance of our God,_
> _to comfort all who mourn,_
> _and provide for those who grieve in Zion—_

to bestow on them a crown of beauty
    instead of ashes,
the oil of gladness
    instead of mourning,
and a garment of praise
    instead of a spirit of despair.
They will be called oaks of righteousness,
    *a planting of the L*ORD
    for the display of his splendor.
—Isaiah 61:1–3

Do you see how much of this description of Messiah's role has to do with comforting?

How have you experienced—or are you experiencing—mourning in your life due to the sorrows life brings us all?

_____

_____

How have you become *"a planting of the L*ORD *for the display of his splendor"*?

_____

_____

Recall what Paul said would be the result of our righteous suffering (Romans 5:2–5). *"We rejoice in the hope of the* _____ _____ *. . . . And hope does not disappoint us."* Do you see a similar message in God's Word from Isaiah?

_____

DAY 5

MAN OF SORROWS, ACQUAINTED WITH GRIEF

"Blessed are those who mourn, for they shall be comforted," Jesus said in His inaugural address. He was describing His own heart, which He would reproduce in His people through the power of His indwelling Spirit. The law on the inside—grace. The mark of those set apart.

At your entrance to the kingdom, when the King comes into your life to rule there, He begins to recreate your heart so that it is the exact reflection of His. Jesus has no sin of His own to mourn over, but He does mourn over your sin. He mourns over your sin because of how deeply He loves you. That which is named by God as "sin" is that which diminishes your life. That's why it is called sin. It hurts you. It causes you harm. It impedes you. Jesus hates sin because Jesus loves you.

When the living, indwelling, present Jesus communicates His heart to you regarding your sin, it is called conviction. Your enemy condemns, but Jesus convicts. Condemnation brings guilt and hopelessness, but conviction brings repentance and restoration. Conviction brings what Paul refers to as *"godly sorrow."*

> *For you became sorrowful as God intended and so were not harmed in any way by us. Godly sorrow brings repentance that leads to salvation and leaves no regret, but worldly sorrow brings death.*
> —2 Corinthians 7:9–11

Jesus's sorrow over your sin, transfused into your heart, results in repentance. Repentance leads to salvation—not just the initial acceptance of eternal salvation, but continual salvation from the sins that have a grip on you. Each experience of conviction that leads to repentance and then leads to freedom allows you to know the comfort of the Father. The full force of the blood of Christ, flowing through you now, washing away your sins—could there be any greater comfort? If you are responding to the enemy's condemnation rather than the Spirit's conviction, the comfort of forgiveness never comes.

Are you experiencing conviction in any area right now? Are you willing to let that godly sorrow bring repentance that leads to salvation?

WEEK TWO

_____

_____

Is there any point at which you have been mistaking the enemy's condemnation for the Spirit's conviction? Listen now to the comfort of the Father.

Jesus also mourns over those caught in sin and needing His salvation.

> *"O Jerusalem, Jerusalem, you who kill the prophets and stone those sent to you, how often I have longed to gather your children together, as a hen gathers her chicks under her wings, but you were not willing. Look, your house is left to you desolate. For I tell you, you will not see me again until you say, 'Blessed is he who comes in the name of the Lord.'"*
> —Matthew 23:37–39

When He looks at those who are blinded by the evil one, trapped in the web of sin and flesh, it arouses sorrow and compassion in Him.

> *When he saw the crowds, he had compassion on them, because they were harassed and helpless, like sheep without a shepherd. Then he said to his disciples, "The harvest is plentiful but the workers are few. Ask the Lord of the harvest, therefore, to send out workers into his harvest field."*
> —Matthew 9:36–38

Not anger or disgust, but compassion. When Jesus is reproducing His heart in you, His compassion and sorrow for those who are lost and going their own way will spill over into your heart. Self-righteousness, anger, bitterness—these are not the responses Christ is forming in you toward nonbelievers who act and think like nonbelievers. *"[M]an's anger does not bring about the righteous life that God desires"* (James 1:20).

When Jesus mourns over those He came to save, He is compelled to go the full distance on their behalf and pour out His life on the Cross to save them. He finds comfort in the Father's assurance that He has completed the work He came to do (John 17:4). Jesus's mourning for the lost is not passive, but redemptive and deliberate and reaching.

Set Apart

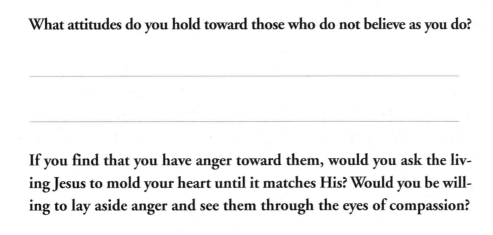

What attitudes do you hold toward those who do not believe as you do?

_____

_____

If you find that you have anger toward them, would you ask the living Jesus to mold your heart until it matches His? Would you be willing to lay aside anger and see them through the eyes of compassion?

_____

_____

Jesus experienced sorrow brought on by circumstances to a level that you and I will never know. Throughout His walk on earth, He experienced rejection, humiliation, betrayal, ridicule, even physical threats. But all that paled in comparison to the agony of the crucifixion.

Let's look at some of the moments of raw and ragged grief glimpsed in the Gospels.

> _"The hour has come for the Son of Man to be glorified. I tell you the truth, unless a kernel of wheat falls to the ground and dies, it remains only a single seed. But if it dies, it produces many seeds. The man who loves his life will lose it, while the man who hates his life in this world will keep it for eternal life. Whoever serves me must follow me; and where I am, my servant also will be. My Father will honor the one who serves me._
>
> _"Now my heart is troubled, and what shall I say? 'Father, save me from this hour'? No, it was for this very reason I came to this hour. Father, glorify your name!"_
> —John 12:23–28

Notice how Jesus opens His remarks. _"The hour has come for the Son of Man to be glorified."_ He could have said, "The hour has come for the Son of Man to be beaten, humiliated, crucified." But, instead, He said, _"The hour has come for the Son of Man to be_ glorified._"_ And the path to glory goes through the Cross.

Go to the last sentences (verses 27 and 28) and get the sense of the sorrow and mourning Jesus is experiencing. His heart is troubled. The Hebrew word Jesus likely used (*dalach*), interpreted by the Greek word *tarasso* in the text, means to be in turmoil, to be churned up, to be agitated. It depicts a storm in the soul. Jesus was not just a little out of sorts. He was in agony.

While He is in mourning and deep distress, He begins to reason out what faith requires of Him. I know He is speaking to His disciples, but I'm guessing that He was talking to Himself as well. Do you ever do that? Reason things out in conversation with someone else? I'm just imagining, but I think I'm not far off the mark.

Examine Jesus's thought processes in John 12 as He works His way through mourning. Why do you think He used the title, Son of Man, in this setting instead of one of His other messianic titles?

_____

_____

Outline His reasoning. He is, I believe, reminding Himself about the purpose and the process of His sacrifice. Getting it all in context because His emotions are roiling. Summarize each point He makes.

The grain that falls into the ground:
The one who loves his life in this world:
Whoever serves Me must follow Me (in obedience):
I'd like to say, "Father, save Me from this hour, but …":
"Father, glorify Yourself":

_____

_____

_____

Set Apart

Comforted to Comfort

Jesus experienced real, honest-to-goodness mourning and sorrow. He wasn't aloof and emotionless. Let's look at another telling moment.

> *"My soul is overwhelmed with sorrow to the point of death. Stay here and keep watch with me."*
>
> *Going a little farther, he fell with his face to the ground and prayed, "My Father, if it is possible, may this cup be taken from me. Yet not as I will, but as you will."...*
>
> *He went away a second time and prayed, "My Father, if it is not possible for this cup to be taken away unless I drink it, may your will be done."*
>
> *When he came back, he again found them sleeping, because their eyes were heavy. So he left them and went away once more and prayed the third time, saying the same thing.*
>
> *Then he returned to the disciples and said to them, "Are you still sleeping and resting? Look, the hour is near, and the Son of Man is betrayed into the hands of sinners. Rise, let us go! Here comes my betrayer!"*
> —Matthew 26:38–39; 42–46

In Gethsemane, Jesus's soul was so overwhelmed with sorrow that He felt He could die from the agony of it. See Him, as He wrestles His humanity into submission to the Father's will. There in the place of prayer, heart poured out like water in the presence of the Lord (Lamentations 2:19), Jesus—Son of Man—reaches the place of steadiness and purposeful peace. Through the rest of His searing ordeal, He was even and controlled and steady. Where did that come from? It came from the garden hours.

His agony, His mourning, His distress, His turmoil—all drove Him to the garden where He found the presence of the Father to be the comfort necessary to march out and engage the enemy on His own terms. *"Rise, let us go! Here comes my betrayer!"*

The comfort Jesus offers is not just a pat on the back or a gesture of goodwill. The comfort that Jesus gives is His very own person living in you, imparting His peace and serenity to you. The peace He sweat drops of blood to find in the garden, He now gives to you.

Blessed be the God and Father of our Lord Jesus Christ, the Father of mercies and God of all comfort, who comforts us in all our affliction so that we will be able to comfort those who are in any affliction with the comfort with which we ourselves are comforted by God. For just as the sufferings

of Christ are ours in abundance, so also our comfort is abundant through Christ.
—2 Corinthians 1:3–5 (NASB)

As you experience the comfort of Jesus in your sorrows, you can pass that along through the power of Christ in you. You will experience the sorrow and the wrestling that goes with surrendering your flesh—your human nature—for crucifixion time and again. But Jesus has already won that battle and found the comfort that shows itself in courage and determined purpose. Let Him impart His hard-won comfort to you. Let Him deposit His comfort right into your heart. Then let it flow from you to those around you. Real comfort for real sorrow.

Comfort and Joy

Though Jesus was familiar with sorrow, the characteristic that most marked Him was joy.

"I have told you this so that my joy may be in you and that your joy may be complete" (John 15:11–12). *"I am coming to you now, but I say these things while I am still in the world, so that they may have the full measure of my joy within them"* (John 17:13–14).

How does that happen? How does a man who knew the deepest sorrow have complete joy—the full measure of joy?

The only way to have the experience of the supernatural comfort of the Father is to mourn. When that comfort meets you and blankets you and invades your life, you know something you can't know any other way. The word *comfort* takes on a whole new definition, but not one that can be put into words. The comfort that grows out of sorrow is unspeakable.

Jesus explained it this way:

"I tell you the truth, you will weep and mourn while the world rejoices. You will grieve, but your grief will turn to joy. A woman giving birth to a child has pain because her time has come; but when her baby is born she forgets the anguish because of her joy that a child is born into the world."
—John 16:20–22

Jesus was speaking to His disciples about what they were about to experience in His short absence—between the Cross and the resurrection. But it is a principle and a pattern for how sorrow leads to comfort and to joy. A joy that was birthed in pain is the sweetest of all.

Blessed are they that mourn, for they will be comforted.

WEEK THREE

DAY 1

BLESSED ARE THE MEEK

Meekness is another word for strength. Meekness can be described as strength under control, like a horse that has been broken and has put its great strength under its trainer's control. True meekness, which comes from a transformed heart, has strength as its bedrock. True meekness, born of strength, might be mimicked in humble-appearing actions, but the heart of meekness must be forged in the fire.

The word *meekness* is a word from which we recoil. As generally used, it smacks of victimhood and weakness. But this clearly is not the implication Jesus intends here. We need to delve into the meaning of meekness as Jesus uses it to describe His own heart and the heart He will produce in His followers—those set apart from the world to serve His purpose.

In this beatitude, Jesus was directly quoting from the Hebrew Scriptures. *"But the meek will inherit the land and enjoy great peace"* (Psalm 37:11). Examining the context of some passages where the word is used will give us a hint as to its meaning.

Use the following passages as reference and mine the meaning of the word *meek*.

*"Then will I purify the lips of the peoples, that all of them may call on the name of the L*ORD
      and serve him shoulder to shoulder.
From beyond the rivers of Cush my worshipers, my scattered people,
      will bring me offerings.
On that day you will not be put to shame for all the wrongs you have done to me,
      because I will remove from this city those who rejoice in their pride.
Never again will you be haughty on my holy hill.
But I will leave within you the meek and humble,
      who trust in the name of the Lord.
The remnant of Israel will do no wrong; they will speak no lies,
      nor will deceit be found in their mouths.
They will eat and lie down and no one will make them afraid."
—Zephaniah 3:9–13

In this passage, the Lord is talking about a time when He will restore His people from oppression and captivity and will make the people holy. Notice first whom He will keep in place. *"But I will leave within you the _____."*

So, *"the meek and humble"* are the remnant and will be the focus of His restoration. Write out all the words and phrases that describe characteristics that God will build into the meek and humble.

_____

_____

_____

_____

WEEK THREE

Write out the characteristics of those who are not meek and humble. What is the opposite of meek and humble?

_____

_____

Those whom the Lord describes as meek and humble trust in ____

_____.

In what or whom do the proud and haughty trust?

_____

How would you synthesize the difference between the meek and humble and the proud and haughty?

_____

_____

Now consider Psalm 37, from which Jesus directly draws this beatitude. He clearly intends for this psalm to define His meaning when he says, *"Blessed are the meek."*

Do not fret because of evil men
    or be envious of those who do wrong;
for like the grass they will soon wither,
    like green plants they will soon die away.

Trust in the LORD *and do good;*
    dwell in the land and enjoy safe pasture.
Delight yourself in the LORD
    and he will give you the desires of your heart.

Commit your way to the LORD;
    trust in him and he will do this:
He will make your righteousness shine like the dawn,
    the justice of your cause like the noonday sun.

Be still before the LORD and wait patiently for him;
    do not fret when men succeed in their ways,
when they carry out their wicked schemes.

Refrain from anger and turn from wrath;
    do not fret—it leads only to evil.
For evil men will be cut off,
    but those who hope in the LORD will inherit the land.

A little while, and the wicked will be no more;
    though you look for them, they will not be found.
But the meek will inherit the land
    and enjoy great peace.
—Psalm 37:1–11

Remember the principle of interpretation called *gezerah shavah* (cut equally)? When matching wording is used in more than one place, it ties one text to the other. Do you see the phrase *"will inherit the land"* twice? Highlight the two uses of the phrase.

Tying those two phrases together, *meek* is synonymous with *"those who _____."*

Make a list of the instructions to the meek scattered throughout this passage.

_____

_____

_____

_____

Would you agree with this summary? The meek put their full trust in the Lord and wait for His work in His way at His time. The meek do not trust in their own ability nor do they act in their own strength.

The Lord knows that it often appears that the loud, brash, and overbearing inherit the land. It sometimes looks like those who trust in themselves win the day. But it is not really so, He says. Pride has in it the seeds of its own destruction. The meek have the strength to wait it out and to let God work. The meek have learned that pride is weakness and meekness is strength.

WEEK THREE

DAY 2

THE MEEKEST MEN

Now Moses was a very humble man, more humble than anyone else on the face of the earth.
—Numbers 12:3

"I am gentle and humble in heart."
—Matthew 11:29

The words translated *humble* in these verses could be translated *meek*. The description of Moses uses the same Hebrew word used in Psalm 37:11. The description of Jesus uses a derivative of the word *meek* from the Beatitudes.

In Jesus's day, the rabbis referred to Moses as "the former redeemer," and they were looking for "the latter redeemer" to appear. Messiah would be the latter redeemer. They expected Messiah to be like Moses. And, as it turned out, He was like Moses. Both had meekness as a strength.

The two pivotal individuals in God's covenant relationship with His people were characterized as meek. Both men upon whom God placed responsibility for ushering in His covenant in the lives of His people were meek. In the two, meekness was not an afterthought, but instead meekness defined them. Moses and Jesus embodied meekness.

The Making of Meekness

Meekness is a work in progress. The flesh—meaning your own human nature operating independently of the Spirit—works against meekness. But God is at work in us developing the strength of meekness. Let's look at Moses's example and see how God used circumstances to mold meekness. I'm going to borrow from my book, *Fueled by Faith*, where I wrote about Moses's transformation.

Moses was among the most powerful men in Egypt—mighty in both word and action; positioned to rule Egypt; strong; handsome; intelligent; and highly educated. Moses had it all.

Moses was also pregnant with promise. An inner vision kept seeping into his thinking and his passions and grew stronger with each passing year. He wanted his Hebrew kinsmen to be free. As the vision gestated and grew more substantive, Moses realized that he wanted to be the one to free them. Then came the day when Moses tried to give birth to the vision prematurely. He tried to induce labor. He murdered an Egyptian taskmaster who was beating a Hebrew slave. At best—if all had gone well—Moses would have temporarily rescued one lone Hebrew. Do you see how far short that falls of the vision that God had in mind? Do you see what a cheap imitation we produce when the vision gets tangled up with our flesh?

When Moses happened upon this incident, he must have thought, "This is my chance. It's now or never. When I strike this blow, all my Hebrew kinsmen will recognize that I can set them free." Notice how Stephen reports it in Acts 7:25. "Moses thought that his own people would realize that God was using him to rescue them, but they did not."

Moses had no qualms about his ability to rescue Israel. He had no doubt that not only could he accomplish it, but also that the people would recognize and embrace him as their rescuer. As the vision grew in Moses until he recognized it and welcomed it, he probably thought, "Of course God has chosen and appointed me to rescue Israel. Who else? I'm the only one who could accomplish it. Anyone can see that I am the man." Moses was absolutely confident in Moses. Moses trusted in Moses.

Then Moses experienced something that he'd never experienced before in his life: failure. humiliation. And he was doing what God had, from all eternity, set him in place to do. But he was doing it in his flesh.

This incident in Moses's life was all part of God's plan for how the vision would develop. Moses's failure was not a setback, but was a step forward in the gestation of the vision. Even our failures, when surrendered to the purposes of God, turn out to be essential to the development of the promise. Because of His failure, Moses's life was open to God for a new work. Now God could take Moses's strength and make it weakness, so that He could take Moses's weakness and make it strength. When we are weak, then we are strong.

When God came to Moses 40 years later, and called him to rescue Israel, the Moses who once thought that it should be obvious to anyone that he was the rescuer no longer lived. A new Moses had been born. This Moses said, "'Who am I, that I should go to Pharaoh and bring the Israelites out of Egypt?' And God said, 'I will be with you'" (Exodus 3:11–12). From that moment, the exodus event emphasizes not who Moses is, but who God is.... He cut away all of Moses's flesh from the promise and left it with nothing but God.

Before the desert, Moses thought himself fully capable of rescuing Israel. The same Moses, after the desert, said, *"Who am I, that I should go?"* In the desert God did a work of crucifixion in Moses. Moses's flesh, with its confidence and pride, died a bloody and painful death. In order to qualify as the meekest man on the face of the earth, Moses had to encounter the power of the Cross in his personality. In linear time, the Cross was in the future. But in eternity, the Cross is always a present reality. The strength of the flesh is always under a death sentence, and God's pattern from beginning to end is to arrange for the execution of flesh in His people so that His power will be in control. His Spirit will be their strength: *"'Not by might nor by power, but by my Spirit,' says the LORD Almighty"* (Zechariah 4:6).

How is Jesus developing meekness in you right now? Are there situations or relationships that are bringing you to the end of yourself? Write out your thoughts about where you are in the process right now.

Meekness on Display

At moments of crisis, when all the defenses are down and intense emotions are engaged, the real person is revealed. When Jesus faced the deepest darkness any person will ever know, when the Cross loomed large on His horizon, when His soul was in such agony that He thought He could die from it—what was revealed? Meekness.

Let's explore two questions: (1) Where was meekness born? (2) What did meekness look like?

Remember Gethsemane. Remember Jesus wrestling with the issue of complete submission to the Father? To be sure, Jesus was without sin. There was no rebellion or resistance to God's will in Him. But He was fully man as well as fully God, and He did have to willfully lay aside the instincts of His human nature to fully embrace His mission. *"Yet not as I will, but as you will"* (Matthew 26:39). Three times He prayed the same way until His humanity had fully surrendered to crucifixion.

Throughout His life on earth, Jesus had always been meek. The incarnation's opening act was a stunning display of meekness. Never anything but meek, Jesus still learned deeper and deeper levels of surrender as deeper surrender was called for. In Gethsemane, the course had been completed, and it was time for the final exam. It was time to show once and for all the fruits of the training.

"Although he was a son, he learned obedience from what he suffered and, once made perfect, he became the source of eternal salvation for all who obey him" (Hebrews 5:8–9). May I paraphrase this? He learned deeper levels of obedience at each stage of His life and once He completed the training ("made perfect" means "brought to completion"), He evidenced His perfect obedience and submission on the Cross.

The ultimate display of His meekness came after Gethsemane. Where was meekness born? In the crucible of His circumstances.

What did meekness look like?

> *He was oppressed and afflicted,*
> *   yet he did not open his mouth;*
> *he was led like a lamb to the slaughter,*
> *   and as a sheep before her shearers is silent,*
> *so he did not open his mouth.*
> —Isaiah 53:7

Jesus left His defense to the Father. Without lashing out or justifying Himself or demanding His rights, He died for the sins of even those who were pounding the nails into His flesh. He forgave even while He was being savagely executed and publicly scorned.

These words sum up the strength of His meekness: *"You would have no power over me if it were not given to you from above"* (John 19:11). His absolute surrender to the Father's will and His absolute dependence on the Father's power were the ultimate display of meekness.

What do you learn about your own life from Jesus's ultimate display of meekness?

Are you willing to let the indwelling Jesus impart His meekness to you?

Matters of Meekness

Jesus expounded on His beatitude about meekness further in the sermon. For example, in the following passage:

> *"You have heard that it was said, 'Eye for eye, and tooth for tooth.' But I tell you, Do not resist an evil person. If someone strikes you on the right cheek, turn to him the other also. And if someone wants to sue you and take your tunic, let him have your cloak as well. If someone forces you to go one mile, go with him two miles. Give to the one who asks you, and do not turn away from the one who wants to borrow from you.*
>
> *"You have heard that it was said, 'Love your neighbor and hate your enemy.' But I tell you: Love your enemies and pray for those who persecute you, that you may be sons of your Father in heaven. He causes his sun to rise on the evil and the good, and sends rain on the righteous and the unrighteous. If you love those who love you, what reward will you get? Are not even the tax collectors doing that? And if you greet only your brothers, what are you doing more than others? Do not even pagans do that? Be perfect, therefore, as your heavenly Father is perfect."*
> —Matthew 5:38–48

As an aside, debate has always accompanied these verses. When to resist, when to give in. Jesus resisted at times, but never on His own behalf. Let me encourage you, for the sake of this lesson, not to get sidetracked into these discussions. Let's just get to the heart of meekness.

In these opening verses, Jesus is describing a situation in which someone has power over you. We hate to feel powerless. It is very hard, in our flesh, to feel subject to another person. The first challenge to the flesh's mastery is to submit to someone's authority, especially if that person has evil motives. But remember these words: *"You would have no power over me if it were not given to you from above"* (John 19:11).

When we are in positions of powerlessness, such as Jesus described, the way of the flesh is to do what has to be done and nothing more, seething on the inside. "I'll show you. You just wait. You'll get yours," go the flesh's thoughts at such a time. The powerful person gains even more power over us because we are letting the poison of bitterness and hatred seep in and begin its destruction. When we respond in the pattern of our flesh, then we are really weak. We are indeed powerless.

But how would meekness meet the challenge? Imagine this scenario. You are powerless. Some evil person whose demands you must obey strikes you on the cheek, or compels you to give up your tunic, or forces you to go a mile with him. These, of course, are all cultural references. They represent the situations you encounter. The meek person is so strong that outward insults and demands that might humiliate a weak person, do not affect the meek person. The meek person does not have to chafe and boil on the inside, giving the offender more power over him. The meek person is so free from the tyranny of his outward circumstances that he is free to cheerfully perform more than duty. He performs ministry. Do you see the principle?

Love your enemy? Impossible for your flesh. Only through grace. Only by the indwelling, present Jesus operating through you. How first to love an enemy? Pray for him. Don't pray that your enemy will change to suit you, or that your enemy will get what he deserves. Pray blessings on anyone who considers himself your enemy. You'll soon find your heart following your prayers. It takes strength to be meek.

Meekness is all about the heart. How does meekness give freedom when those around you are mistreating you?

_____

_____

Does a specific current circumstance come to your mind as you think about these principles? What is the Lord telling you?

_____

DAY 3

THEY WILL INHERIT THE LAND

All the promises that accompany the Beatitudes are different ways of promising the kingdom. Your translation might say that the meek will inherit the earth, but the word is the *land*. In Hebrew thought, *the land* can only mean one thing: Canaan, the Promised Land. The land where all God's power and provision are available. The meek inherit the land. *Inherit* is the word used in the Old Testament to describe Israel's possession of Canaan. It means to take possession of. The root of the word means to take possession of property through a will or as an inheritance. Think about an inheritance. How does a person become an heir to an inheritance? By being born. The heir possesses his inheritance by virtue of relationship. He did not own it or earn it. It was given to him because of whose he is.

The meek will inherit the land. The kingdom is given to them because they are the King's. "The land" in the Old Testament becomes "the kingdom" in the New Testament.

"The righteous will inherit the land and dwell in it forever" (Psalm 37:29). *"Those the LORD blesses will inherit the land"* (Psalm 37:22).

The Hebrew people knew that the land was the blessing. The land was where the abundance waited. The land was the place where rest was theirs. The land was ruled by the King's rules.

> *"'Follow my decrees and be careful to obey my laws, and you will live safely in the land. Then the land will yield its fruit, and you will eat your fill and live there in safety.'"*
> —Leviticus 25:18–19

The kingdom is the land. The dimension of our reality where heaven provides for earth's needs.

Blessed are those who look only to the Lord and His strength and who have surrendered the strength of their flesh for the power of the Spirit. Blessed are those who are so anchored in the indwelling Christ that outward events do not distress them or give openings for bitterness to take root. They live in the land of abundant supply.

But blessed is the man who trusts in the Lord,
    whose confidence is in him.
He will be like a tree planted by the water
    that sends out its roots by the stream.
It does not fear when heat comes;
    its leaves are always green.
It has no worries in a year of drought
    and never fails to bear fruit.
—Jeremiah 17:7–8

Blessed are the meek, for they will inherit the land.

DAY 4

BLESSED ARE THOSE WHO HUNGER AND THIRST FOR RIGHTEOUSNESS

The Greek word translated as "hunger and thirst" means "to avidly desire something as necessary to life." This Greek word is likely interpreting the Hebrew word that means "an acute lack of food." It can also be used for the exhaustion caused by a military campaign or a desert journey, according to Eerdmans *Theological Dictionary of the New Testament*.

Blessed are those who are famished and desperate and ravenous for righteousness. Blessed are those who are consumed with a desire for righteousness. Blessed are those who crave righteousness.

The desire for righteousness is compared to the body's craving for food and drink. Why does the body crave food and drink? Because the body is created so that it requires food and drink to sustain life. Your body is fueled by food and drink, and in their absence it will quit functioning and die.

Why do God's people hunger and thirst for righteousness? Because we are created to be righteous. The word *righteous* means "to be right." It means to have everything functioning well. When we are righteous, then we are satisfied, and our deepest longings are fulfilled. Like everything else He gives, righteousness is not a gift apart from Himself. He gives us Himself—the law on the inside, grace, Christ in you—and in Him is everything. The longing for righteousness comes from Him. The gift of His righteousness comes from Him.

Take some time right now to let the living and active Word of God stir longing in your heart for the presence of God. Make these words your own heart's cry. Highlight words that speak of intensity and desire. Soak your heart in these words until you feel the hunger.

God, you are my God,
*   earnestly I seek you;*
my soul thirsts for you,
*   my body longs for you,*
in a dry and weary land
*   where there is no water.*

I have seen you in the sanctuary
*   and beheld your power and your glory.*
Because your love is better than life,
*   my lips will glorify you.*
I will praise you as long as I live,
*   and in your name I will lift up my hands.*
My soul will be satisfied as with the richest of foods;
*   with singing lips my mouth will praise you.*

On my bed I remember you;
*   I think of you through the watches of the night.*
Because you are my help,
*   I sing in the shadow of your wings.*
My soul clings to you;
*   your right hand upholds me.*
—**Psalm 63:1–8**

As the deer pants for streams of water,
*   so my soul pants for you, O God.*
My soul thirsts for God, for the living God.
*   When can I go and meet with God?*
—**Psalm 42:1–2**

My soul is consumed with longing
*   for your laws at all times.*
…
How I long for your precepts!
…
My soul faints with longing for your salvation,
*   but I have put my hope in your word.*
…
I open my mouth and pant,
*   longing for your commands.*
…
I rejoice in your promise
*   like one who finds great spoil.*
…
I long for your salvation, O LORD,
*   and your law is my delight.*
—**Psalm 119:20, 40, 81, 131, 162, 174**

WEEK THREE

Day 4: Blessed Are Those Who Hunger and Thirst for Righteousness

Notice how often the Scripture uses the metaphor of food for God's Word.

"It is written: 'Man does not live on bread alone, but on every word that comes from the mouth of God.'"
—Matthew 4:4

"Come, all you who are thirsty, come to the waters;
  and you who have no money, come, buy and eat!
Come, buy wine and milk without money and without cost.
Why spend money on what is not bread,
  and your labor on what does not satisfy?
Listen, listen to me, and eat what is good,
  and your soul will delight in the richest of fare."
—Isaiah 55:1–2

And he said to me, "Son of man, eat what is before you, eat this scroll; then go and speak to the house of Israel." So I opened my mouth, and he gave me the scroll to eat. Then he said to me, "Son of man, eat this scroll I am giving you and fill your stomach with it." So I ate it, and it tasted as sweet as honey in my mouth.
—Ezekiel 3:1–3

Jesus speaks of the one who hungers and thirsts for righteousness. The Scripture calls us to consider the Word of God as nourishment for our spirits in the same way that food is nourishment for our bodies. Could it be that feasting continually on the Word of God is the first step to experiencing the righteousness that Christ imparts within us?

The Scripture is God's Word. Jesus is the Living Word, the Word embodied, and He lives in me. I think about it like this: Jesus, present with me and in me eternally, breaks the bread of the Word and feeds it to me, bite by bite. Like food in my body, it is digested and made available to my spirit, to my mind, to my emotions. I absorb it into my soul's cells where it releases power and cleansing and nourishment and growth.

The Word of God does more than inform. It transforms. It renews the mind. It restores the soul. It energizes and motivates and corrects. Without a continual feeding on His Word, you will waste away.

The first step in satisfying that hunger for righteousness is to let the Word of God feed you and find that it increases your appetite.

Food You Know Not Of

Jesus spoke of the Father's will as food. During His encounter with the woman at the well in Samaria (John 4:1–34), His disciples had left to get food for Him. They had been traveling, and the road they were traveling was arduous. He was at the well that day at that time because He was tired and hungry and thirsty. While His disciples were gone, He had this transforming encounter with the Samaritan woman, with whom He had a conversation about water.

> There came a woman of Samaria to draw water. Jesus said to her, "Give Me a drink."
>
> For His disciples had gone away into the city to buy food.
>
> Therefore the Samaritan woman said to Him, "How is it that You, being a Jew, ask me for a drink since I am Samaritan woman?" (For Jews have no dealings with Samaritans.)
>
> Jesus answered and said to her, "If you knew the gift of God, and who it is who says to you, 'Give Me a drink,' you would have asked Him, and He would have given you living water."
>
> She said to Him, "Sir, You have nothing to draw with and the well is deep; where then do You get that living water? You are not greater than our father Jacob, are You, who gave us the well, and drank of it himself and his sons and his cattle?"
>
> Jesus answered and said to her, "Everyone who drinks of this water will thirst again; but whoever drinks of the water that I will give him shall never thirst; but the water that I will give him will become in him a well of water springing up to eternal life."
>
> The woman said to Him, "Sir, give me this water, so I will not be thirsty nor come all the way here to draw."
>
> —John 4:7–15 (NASB)

How efficiently timed this was. Had the disciples been present, the woman may not have come, or at least she might not have been as open. But, as God's perfect timing would have it, she was at the right place at the right time for a face-to-face encounter with Jesus.

I love this story because I think we get a glimpse into how much Jesus loved ministry. He got so caught up in interacting with the Samaritan woman about eternal matters that He seems to have forgotten all about His thirst. His thirst for righteousness overpowered His physical thirst.

His disciples returned with the food they had brought Him and encouraged Him to eat. Remember, before they left He had been hungry.

But he said to them, "I have food to eat that you know nothing about."

Then his disciples said to each other, "Could someone have brought him food?"

"My food," said Jesus, "is to do the will of him who sent me and to finish his work.
—John 4:32–34

He was so filled spiritually by His ministry to the woman He met at the well that His physical hunger disappeared. Doing His Father's will filled and energized Him. *"For the kingdom of God is not a matter of eating and drinking, but of righteousness, peace and joy in the Holy Spirit"* (Romans 14:17–18).

Could it be that another way to fill our hunger and thirst for righteousness is to simply be obedient every moment to the Father's will? This kind of obedience will require that we are always in step with the Spirit and alert to His whispers. Jesus is reproducing His obedience in us every second of every day.

To recap, feasting on the Word and being obedient to the Father's will are responses to our craving for righteousness. These things don't make us righteous, but they do open the door so that the Righteous One has access to our hearts where He can do His work.

Ask the living, indwelling Jesus to create in you even greater appetite for righteousness.

What are some things the Spirit is bringing to mind that might suppress your appetite for righteousness?

_____

_____

What are the things that stir up your appetite for righteousness?

_____

_____

DAY 5

ONLY ONE IS RIGHTEOUS

Jesus is righteousness. He is our righteousness.

Because He made Himself an offering for my sin, He made me right with God. Because He lives in me now, directing my life and transforming my motivations and renewing my thought processes, He is progressively making me righteous in my behavior. It is His power working in me to accomplish what I cannot. That includes stirring up my appetite for righteousness.

Have you ever noticed that nothing awakens your appetite like the aroma of a favorite food? Aroma immediately creates desire and then craving. Did you know that God spreads the aroma of Christ through His people? (See 2 Corinthians 2:14–16). One way to get your appetite revved up is to be closely aligned and in fellowship with other believers.

Activity arouses hunger. After a strenuous day, your appetite might be in overdrive. You can hardly wait to get food and drink. The Scripture calls us to labor in the power and the energy of Christ in us: *"We proclaim him, admonishing and teaching everyone with all wisdom, so that we may present everyone perfect in Christ. To this end I labor, struggling with all his energy, which so powerfully works in me"* (Colossians 1:28–29).

I want to have my appetite for righteousness increased because His filling will be in direct proportion to my desiring.

They Shall Be Filled

Those who hunger for righteousness shall be filled. Filled with what? Filled with righteousness. The hunger, like physical hunger, is ongoing. The filling is ongoing. Ever more hungry, ever more full. Jesus is filling us with Himself, and with His righteousness.

> *For in Christ all the fullness of the Deity lives in bodily form, and you have been given fullness in Christ, who is the head over every power and authority.*
> —Colossians 2:9–11

> *That you may be filled to the measure of all the fullness of God.*
> —Ephesians 3:19

God wants you full. *Blessed are those who hunger and thirst after righteousness, for they shall be filled.*

WEEK FOUR

DAY 1

BLESSED ARE THE MERCIFUL

Mercy acts. It is love compelled into action. More than a feeling. More than an attitude or an outlook. Mercy is compassion that is driven to rescue and defend.

Rabbi Jesus, continuing His description of the heart He will reproduce in His disciples, declares: *"Blessed are the merciful, for they shall be shown mercy"* (Matthew 5:7). The depth of the meaning of the Greek root word used here for "mercy," *eleos*, may be found in the Hebrew word *rachmani*, which Jesus likely used when he delivered his sermon. This word, *rachmani*, implies a deep love (as in a parent to a child) and is sometimes translated "compassion" or "pity." It has the sense of active empathy—to feel what another is feeling.

The same Greek root word is found also in the Book of Hebrews.

For this reason he had to be made like his brothers in every way, in order that he might become a merciful and faithful high priest in service to God, and that he might make atonement for the sins of the people. Because he himself suffered when he was tempted, he is able to help those who are being tempted.
—**Hebrews 2:17–18**

What do you see in this description of Jesus that hints at the full meaning of mercy?

_____

_____

_____

_____

The Hebrew word *rachmani* is the root of a word often translated "womb" (*rechem*). Mercy is pictured by the womb, cherishing the fetus. Protective, deeply loving, providing for every need. The strong defending the weak.

Mercy—compassion, pity—is often described in the context of a parent's love for a child.

> *Can a mother forget the baby at her breast*
> *and have no compassion (racham) on the child she has borne?*
> *Though she may forget, I will not forget you!*
> *See, I have engraved you on the palms of my hands;*
> *your walls are ever before me.*
> —Isaiah 49:15–16

> *"I will extend peace to her like a river,*
> *and the wealth of nations like a flooding stream;*

you will nurse and be carried on her arm
and dandled on her knees.
As a mother comforts her child,
so will I comfort you;
and you will be comforted over Jerusalem."
—Isaiah 66:12–13

The kind of love that Jesus is describing when He says, *"Blessed are the merciful,"* is a love that takes responsibility for the plight of someone else. The merciful do not walk away from or close their ears to cries for help. The merciful feel the pain of others as their own.

Look at these passages describing Jesus's heart. *Compassion* is a synonym for *mercy*. From this glimpse, how would you define *mercy*?

Jesus went through all the towns and villages, teaching in their synagogues, preaching the good news of the kingdom and healing every disease and sickness. When he saw the crowds, he had compassion on them, because they were harassed and helpless, like sheep without a shepherd. Then he said to his disciples, "The harvest is plentiful but the workers are few. Ask the Lord of the harvest, therefore, to send out workers into his harvest field."
—Matthew 9:35–38

When Jesus landed and saw a large crowd, he had compassion on them and healed their sick.
—Matthew 14:14

_____

_____

_____

_____

WEEK FOUR

Day 2

Merciful Savior

Mercy has another layer. Mercy suspends judgment. Mercy metes out compassion, not retribution.

The LORD is compassionate and gracious,
slow to anger and abounding in lovingkindness.
He will not always strive with us,
Nor will He keep His anger forever.
He has not dealt with us according to our sins,
Nor rewarded us according to our iniquities.
For as high as the heavens are above the earth,
So great is His lovingkindness toward those who fear Him.
As far as the east is from the west,
So far has he removed our transgressions from us.
Just as a father has compassion on his children,
So the LORD has compassion on those who fear Him.
For He Himself knows our frame;
He is mindful that we are but dust.
—Psalm 103:8–14 (NASB)

Yet he was merciful;
*   he forgave their iniquities*
*   and did not destroy them.*
Time after time he restrained his anger
*   and did not stir up his full wrath.*
He remembered that they were but flesh,
*   a passing breeze that does not return.*
—Psalm 78:38–39

When the Scriptures describe God's mercy and compassion, we see that He looks compassionately upon our weakness. He is patient and restrained in His dealing with us. Even when He corrects, it is His mercy, redirecting us and bringing us back home. It is His mercy that rescues us from the destructive power of our rebellion and sin.

My son, do not despise the LORD's discipline
    and do not resent his rebuke,
because the LORD disciplines those he loves,
    as a father the son he delights in.
—Proverbs 3:11–12

And you have forgotten that word of encouragement that addresses you as
sons:
    "My son, do not make light of the Lord's discipline,
    and do not lose heart when he rebukes you,
    because the Lord disciplines those he loves,
    and he punishes everyone he accepts as a son."
    Endure hardship as discipline; God is treating you as sons... Our
fathers disciplined us for a little while as they thought best; but God dis-
ciplines us for our good, that we may share in his holiness. No discipline
seems pleasant at the time, but painful. Later on, however, it produces a
harvest of righteousness and peace for those who have been trained by it.
—Hebrews 12:5–7, 10–11

Recall that the concept of mercy is described in Scripture as the feeling a parent has toward a child. Looking at the passages from Hebrews and Proverbs, quoted above, how do you see mercy described?

_____

_____

What would you say is the difference between discipline and punishment?

_____

_____

_____

_____

WEEK FOUR

What does discipline produce?

_____

_____

_____

_____

⅍ ⅍ ⅍

Mercy always has redemption as its goal. What will redeem and restore and heal? That is the course mercy will take. Mercy never acts based on what another person deserves. *"He does not treat us as our sins deserve or repay us according to our iniquities"* (Psalm 103:10).

Grace gives us what we don't deserve. Mercy withholds what we do deserve. Two parts of a whole that describe our compassionate Savior, whose heart is being formed in you.

Mercy in Motion

The Life Giver

As the leper struggled through the crowd, his bell announced his shame. "Unclean. Unclean." All the clean ones moved away, avoiding his pain at all costs. The leper worked his way through the religious throng, desperate to find the presence of Jesus.

Jesus looked past his rotting flesh and saw the hope that sloughed away with every rejection, every head that turned away, every face that registered disgust and fear.

Jesus looked past the stench of decaying skin and saw the little spark of life crusted over with loneliness and hurt, almost extinguished.

He heard the anguished cry: *"If you are willing, you can make me clean."* He restored the leper's disease-ravaged body, but more than that, He restored his shame-ravaged soul. The fearless, compassionate touch of the Savior clothed the man in dignity. Jesus gave him more than a reprieve from death. Jesus gave him LIFE. (See Matthew 8:1–3.)

The Restorer

They hauled her through the streets, her guilt on display for all to see. No place for her to hide, no shelter from accusing glances and condemning words. She was a perfect target for their collective righteous outrage. A perfect target for the stones they itched to throw.

They dragged her into the presence of Jesus. Just how far would He carry His theme of mercy and compassion? Surely this woman would find mercy's limits. Surely He would have no choice but to join them in their stone-throwing censure.

In Jesus's presence, the stone-throwers discovered that His compassion never fails, His mercies never come to an end. He unmasked the surface righteousness of her accusers and set her free—FORGIVEN. (See John 8:2–11.)

The Heart Cleanser

He was so close, and yet He might as well have been a world away. To reach the presence of Jesus, she would have to wade through the conglomerate of very, very religious ones—the perfectly righteous men—who were His dinner companions today. She would drown in their scorn. Surely she could not keep her head above the waves of their belittling hatred, which were sure to swallow her up. So close! So close!

The longing could not be contained. She had seen the mercy in His eyes when they fell on her that day. He didn't say a word. No one knew but her. When she read the forgiveness in His face, saw the mercy in His glance, she had been born again. A clean slate. A fresh start. A heart flushed out and free of sin's debris. Healed from wounds that festered in her soul. New.

Whatever it took, she would bring Him her most precious possession. She would break it at His feet and pour out everything she owned as her worship and adoration. She would wash His feet with her tears, as He had washed her heart with His mercy.

Breaking through the rigid righteousness of the religious, she found the gentle mercy of the Savior. At Jesus's feet, she who had come to lower herself in His presence, found herself lifted up in the presence of her enemies. She left that day, CLEAN. (See Luke 7:36–50.)

In the many accounts of Jesus's mercy recorded in the Gospels, I notice a thread. Who most often stands in the way of mercy? Who crowds out sinners longing for a Savior?

Do you see any tendencies in your own life or behavior that might discourage someone who is not at ease in religious settings or around religious people?

_____

_____

_____

What does it say about the demeanor of Jesus that outcasts and sinners would brave humiliation and fear to reach Him?

_____

_____

_____

Do you think your life portrays the merciful heart of Jesus?

_____

_____

_____

DAY 3

BECOMING MERCIFUL

Remember, to live in a state of blessedness means to be so fully supplied by Christ in you that you are not captive to circumstances. The law has moved to the inside where it is transforming your heart and, so, conforming your behavior. The law is now the matrix in which your heart is at home.

The Beatitudes—the introduction to King Jesus's inaugural address—are a description of the heart that produces the behaviors the law commands. The Beatitudes are the promise of what Jesus is willing to produce in you as you yield your heart to Him.

The great expositor D. Martyn Lloyd-Jones put it this way:

> His Spirit controls me at the very centre of my life, controls the very spring of my being, the source of my every activity. You cannot read these Beatitudes without coming to that conclusion. The Christian faith is not something on the surface of a man's life, it is not merely a kind of coating or veneer. No, it is something that has been happening in the very centre of his personality.
> —*Studies in the Sermon on the Mount*

The mercy and compassion that are the defining qualities of Jesus's character will be expressed through you. As you yield yourself ever more fully to Him, mercy becomes your natural response.

How does Jesus expound the concept of mercy in the Sermon on the Mount? Take a hint from the parallel speech patterns. *"Blessed are the merciful, for they will be shown mercy."* Compare that to: *"Do not judge, or you too will be judged. For in the same way you judge others, you will be judged, and with the measure you use, it will be measured to you"* (Matthew 7:1–2). Jesus goes on, then, to elaborate.

> *"Why do you look at the speck of sawdust in your brother's eye and pay no attention to the plank in your own eye? How can you say to your brother, 'Let me take the speck out of your eye,' when all the time there is a plank in your own eye? You hypocrite, first take the plank out of your own eye, and then you will see clearly to remove the speck from your brother's eye."*
> —Matthew 7:3–5

These statements would not have been new to the people. They are familiar rabbinic statements, as are many of Jesus's sayings. Jesus is not throwing out the law, and in many cases, concurs with the rabbinical teachings on the law, called the Talmud. Jesus is agreeing with the Talmudic teaching and endorsing it.

> *Do not think that I have come to abolish the Law or the Prophets; I have not come to abolish them but to fulfill them. I tell you the truth, until heaven and earth disappear, not the smallest letter, not the least stroke of a pen, will by any means disappear from the Law until everything is accomplished. Anyone who breaks one of the least of these commandments and teaches others to do the same will be called least in the kingdom of heaven, but whoever practices and teaches these commands will be called great in the kingdom of heaven. For I tell you that unless your righteousness surpasses that of the Pharisees and the teachers of the law, you will certainly not enter the kingdom of heaven.*
> —Matthew 5:17–20

In this passage, Jesus is again using familiar rabbinical language. The rabbis had many parables and proverbs that indicated that neither the smallest Hebrew letter (*yodh*) nor even the small markings that accent letters (*kotz*) would ever be changed in Torah. This was a familiar way to express this reality. The Talmud has many quotations about the speck in one person's eye and a beam in the other's.

> Rabbi Yochanan explained what is the meaning of the words, "And it came to pass, in the days when the judges judged…" (Ruth 1:1). It means that this was a generation in which the judges passed judgment upon each other. If the judge said to a person, "Take the splinter from between your teeth," that person would respond, by saying, "Take the log out of your eye." (*b. Baha Batra* 15 b).
> —Brad H. Young, *Meet the Rabbis*

Familiar language. Jesus standing behind the Torah and the Talmud both.

His statement—*"Anyone who breaks one of the least of these commandments and teaches others to do the same will be called least in the kingdom of heaven, but whoever practices and teaches these commands will be called great in the kingdom of heaven"*—was yet another common saying. The rabbis taught that "light" commandments were as binding as "heavy" commandments. Jesus, using the familiar Hebrew terms, was making a pun. "Anyone who teaches others to break a light commandment will be a lightweight in the kingdom."

Again we see that He is not changing the content of the law, but the location of the law. *"Unless your righteousness surpasses that of the Pharisees and the teachers of the law, you will certainly not enter the kingdom of heaven."* The Pharisees obeyed scrupulously the outward and ceremonial forms of the law, but their hearts were so unbowed that they did not recognize He to whom the law had always pointed.

Jesus stated that He had come to fulfill the law. Brad Young in *Meet the Rabbis* writes that Jesus likely used a typical Hebrew expression (*kiyem*) that means "to interpret the message accurately and to live out the meaning of the law in practice." For a person's righteousness to exceed that of the Pharisees and teachers of the law, that righteousness would have to be deeper. A righteousness of the heart. No one could outdo the Pharisees in the outward forms of religion.

Jesus, borrowing from familiar Talmudic sources, more fully defines mercy as forgoing the judgment that springs so naturally from our flesh. Don't rush to judgment. Don't judge the heart that you can't see. Don't immediately ascribe wrong motives. Give the best interpretation to another's actions, not the worst.

He illustrates by saying, *"Why do you look at the speck of sawdust in your brother's eye and pay no attention to the plank in your own eye?"* Think about it. What would it take to find the speck in someone's eye? You would have to be looking for it. Looking carefully. You would have to be scrutinizing your brother, examining him, expecting to find something. All that time and energy watching your brother or sister for flaws would deflect your attention from your own sins.

What is a natural reaction to a person who is critical and accusing? If you are judgmental, others will likely be judgmental toward you as a form of self-preservation. But, if instead, you extend mercy, then others are likely to extend mercy to you. It seems that mercy begets mercy.

They Shall Be Shown Mercy

The disciple in whom Rabbi Jesus is producing holiness knows firsthand that she has been the recipient of mercy on a grand scale. Megamercy. Comprehensive, macrolevel mercy. Big, big mercy. How can that person respond in any other way? Wouldn't that person be so full of mercy poured in, that mercy would have to pour out? Mercy in, mercy out.

Mercy can be contagious. It usually is. A person who gives mercy, gets mercy. With the measure you use, it will be measured to you. In the kingdom, mercy flows. From the King to the inhabitants of the land. From person to person. In, through, around, between. Mercy floods the land.

What evidence do you see in your life that mercy is becoming your natural response?

_____

_____

Where do you see that you are extending judgment instead of mercy?

_____

_____

In light of the beatitude we are studying what do these words mean to you? *"Be kind and compassionate to one another, forgiving each other, just as in Christ God forgave you"* (Ephesians 4:32).

_____

_____

DAY 4

BLESSED ARE THE PURE IN HEART

Purity is all or nothing. While 99 $^{44}/_{100}$ percent pure might work for Ivory soap, it doesn't work for the heart. Pure or impure—either/or. Almost pure is impure.

When Rabbi Jesus spoke of *purity* in His Jewish setting, the word had a singular meaning to His audience. It was not a nuanced word, but rather a word with a clear and precise meaning. Jesus probably referenced the Hebrew word *tahor,* meaning "ritually clean, set apart for use in worship." In Israel's parlance there was "clean" (pure) and "unclean" (impure). Other societies might declare things "good" or "bad," but Israel declared things "clean" or "unclean"—"pure" or "impure."

Tahor means to be declared pure because the proper rituals have been adhered to. It means to be recognized as pure and ready to be used by God for His purposes. Some purification rituals were preparatory—to make a person ready to encounter God. Other rituals were expiatory—to restore a person to a state of purity after the person had sinned or in some way been ritually defiled. In each case, the purification involved blood.

When Moses had proclaimed every commandment of the law to all the people, he took the blood of calves, together with water, scarlet wool and branches of hyssop, and sprinkled the scroll and all the people. He said, "This is the blood of the covenant, which God has commanded you to keep." In the same way, he sprinkled with the blood both the tabernacle and everything used in its ceremonies. In fact, the law requires that nearly everything be cleansed with blood, and without the shedding of blood there is no forgiveness.
—Hebrews 9:19–22

Preparatory—Before its use, every article in the tabernacle had to be made pure by the sprinkling of blood. The concept was that blood would absorb the pollution that entered the tabernacle between ceremonies. Blood had (symbolically and ritually) the power to absorb sin. Blood, as God placed it in creation, perfectly mirrors its ritual use. Blood absorbs toxins and washes them away. (See my book *The Life-Changing Power in the Blood of Christ* to learn more about this important topic.)

Expiatory—Then, after those articles were purified for use, blood was offered on the altar, and once a year on the mercy seat, for the sins of the people. The blood of the sacrifices cleansed the people from their sins. *"Because on this day atonement will be made for you, to cleanse you. Then, before the LORD, you will be clean from all your sins"* (Leviticus 16:30).

People who had become ritually unclean by their own sin, through disease, or through any number of other ways, were cleansed through ceremonies that required the shedding of blood. Israelites well understood the power of blood to cleanse and purify. Other elements, like oil and water, were used as part of certain cleansing rituals, but blood was the constant.

The shed blood of the sacrificial offering was sprinkled on the person or on the instrument or on the article. By the blood of the pure and innocent life that had been offered for the sins of the people, the people were made ritually clean. Not really clean. Not heart-clean. But God accepted the ceremony until the reality was revealed.

The writer of the Book of Hebrews lays out how the symbolism of the Old Covenant has become the reality under Christ. For example:

The blood of goats and bulls and the ashes of a heifer sprinkled on those who are ceremonially unclean sanctify them so that they are outwardly clean. How much more, then, will the blood of Christ, who through the eternal Spirit offered himself unblemished to God, cleanse our consciences from acts that lead to death, so that we may serve the living God!
—Hebrews 9:13–14

When Moses had proclaimed every commandment of the law to all the people, he took the blood of calves, together with water, scarlet wool and branches of hyssop, and sprinkled the scroll and all the people. He said, "This is the blood of the covenant, which God has commanded you to keep." In the same way, he sprinkled with the blood both the tabernacle and everything used in its ceremonies. In fact, the law requires that nearly everything be cleansed with blood, and without the shedding of blood there is no forgiveness.
—Hebrews 9:19–22

Let us draw near to God with a sincere heart in full assurance of faith, having our hearts sprinkled to cleanse us from a guilty conscience and having our bodies washed with pure water.
—Hebrews 10:22

A clean heart will have to be sprinkled with the blood of the Eternal Sacrifice to cleanse it. A clean heart is not possible unless there is direct contact with blood. The blood of Christ, poured *out* for our sins, but poured *in* for our righteousness. It must have access to our hearts. It must flow—a living fountain opened in the heavenly realms to cleanse and purify the people of God.

A Clean Heart

The Hebrew language is picturesque. Each letter is a picture and when the pictures are combined, they tell a story. Each root word gives the underlying meaning to its derivatives. The Hebrew letters that make up the root word for "pure" picture a basket or container and a man. The root means "to contain a man," according to Jeff Benner's *The Ancient Hebrew Lexicon of the Bible*. It was commonly understood that God's laws and instructions were for man's good and for his protection. They were to "contain" his natural impulses and keep him from destroying himself. *"I will walk about in freedom, for I have sought out your precepts"* (Psalm 119:45).

Jesus's audience was familiar with the Old Testament's use of the word *tahor* to describe the heart that God desired. *"Create in me a pure [clean] heart, O God, and renew a steadfast spirit within me"* (Psalm 51:10, author's insertion). God's call for a pure heart connected with His audience. They knew that it was to their benefit to have a heart cleansed of any pollution.

The religious leaders of the day had lost sight of the clear teaching of the Scriptures they so revered, as well as the oral traditions of the rabbis and sages through the ages. They had fixated on the external ceremonies of cleansing—those things that could be measured and graded and displayed in public. Many of the more prominent leaders seemed to be more concerned about how they were viewed by others than whether or not their hearts were pure. They used the outward expressions of piety and holiness to protect their social position and their authority. They used their superior knowledge of the minutiae of the oral traditions to lord it over the common and uneducated.

Jesus rebuked them publicly, drawing their anger. A public challenge to their law-keeping did not go unnoticed by the people.

"Woe to you, teachers of the law and Pharisees, you hypocrites! You clean the outside of the cup and dish, but inside they are full of greed and self-indulgence. Blind Pharisee! First clean the inside of the cup and dish, and then the outside also will be clean.

"Woe to you, teachers of the law and Pharisees, you hypocrites! You are like whitewashed tombs, which look beautiful on the outside but on the inside are full of dead men's bones and everything unclean. In the same way, on the outside you appear to people as righteous but on the inside you are full of hypocrisy and wickedness."
—Matthew 23:25–28

Day 4: Blessed Are the Pure in Heart

Of course, we know this rebuke came later in His ministry. But the Beatitudes He laid out in His inaugural address were to be lived out and exemplified—fleshed out, you might say—in the rest of His ministry. In this sermon, He told His audience that their righteousness would have to exceed that of the scribes and Pharisees. It would have to go deeper. It would have to reach all the way to the heart.

He said that if the inside is clean, the outside will be clean also. Repeating His theme that when the law is moved to the inside, the outside naturally conforms. When the law transforms the heart, the heart transforms the behavior.

From the following statements, identify the role the heart plays in our actions.

*Though you probe my heart and examine me at night,
    though you test me, you will find nothing;
    I have resolved that my mouth will not sin.*
—Psalm 17:3

*May the words of my mouth and the meditation of my heart
    be pleasing in your sight,
    O LORD, my Rock and my Redeemer.*
—Psalm 19:14

*Who may ascend the hill of the LORD?
    Who may stand in his holy place?
He who has clean hands and a pure heart,
    who does not lift up his soul to an idol
    or swear by what is false.*
—Psalm 24:3–4

*Test me, O LORD, and try me,
    examine my heart and my mind.*
—Psalm 26:2

*Search me, O God, and know my heart;
    test me and know my anxious thoughts.
See if there is any offensive way in me,
    and lead me in the way everlasting.*
—Psalm 139:23–24

Set Apart

WEEK FOUR

"These people come near to me with their mouth
and honor me with their lips,
but their hearts are far from me.
Their worship of me
is made up only of rules taught by men."
—Isaiah 29:13

Rend your heart
and not your garments.
Return to the LORD your God,
for he is gracious and compassionate,
slow to anger and abounding in love,
and he relents from sending calamity.
—Joel 2:13

King of Hearts

In Hebrew, the heart is the inner man—intellect, emotions, and volition. It is the seat of his decision making. The picture created by the Hebrew letters in the word translated "heart" (*lev*) is developed from the first letter, which represents a staff (authority) and the second letter which represents a house or tent (within): the authority within, according to *The Living Words—Volume One* by Jeff Benner. We would better understand it by translating the word as "mind."

The word for "pure" (*tahor*) is often used to describe the gold, silver, or other metals to be used in the tabernacle. In that sense, it has the meaning of "unalloyed" or "unmixed."

The crucible for silver and the furnace for gold, but the LORD tests the heart. —**Proverbs 17:3**

What is this Scripture indicating about the heart? In what way is the heart pictured by gold and silver?

_____

_____

❧ ❧ ❧

The philosopher-theologian Sören Kierkegaard famously said, "Purity of heart is to will one thing." An unalloyed heart does not have any mixture of affection or loyalty. It belongs wholly to the Lord.

> _Teach me your way, O LORD,_
> _   and I will walk in your truth;_
> _give me an undivided heart,_
> _   that I may fear your name._
> _I will praise you, O LORD my God,_
> _   with all my heart;_
> _I will glorify your name forever._
> —Psalm 86:11–12

This is the summation of the law. If the law were to be condensed to one thing, it would be to love the Lord with everything you are. Jesus said:

> _"'Love the Lord your God with all your heart and with all your soul and with all your mind.' This is the first and greatest commandment. And the second is like it: 'Love your neighbor as yourself.' All the Law and the Prophets hang on these two commandments."_
> —Matthew 22:37–40

The first, the great commandment is to love the Lord your God with your whole self. The second flows from it. If you love the Lord fully with an undivided heart, then you will love your neighbor as He does. Without mixture of motive or focus, Christ in you will be reproducing His heart toward your neighbor. Rabbi Jesus, who calls you to a pure heart, creates a pure heart in you.

In David's prayer from Psalm 51:10, as he prays for a clean heart, he also prays for a steadfast spirit. _"Create in me a clean heart, O God, and renew a steadfast spirit within me"_ (Psalm 51:10). The spirit, when used of man's spirit, refers to the inner man and could be a substitute word for "heart."

The word translated "right" means to be steadfast, fixed, immovable. The Hebrew letters tell the story of a seed opening (an open palm and a seed). The seed opens to put down roots and give the plant a foundation and a base (Jeff Benner's *The Ancient Hebrew Lexicon of the Bible*). A pure heart, a steadfast spirit.

In Hebrew poetry it is typical to say the same thing twice, using different words for the same thought. How do these two lines say the same thing? Sum up the full thought put forth by the double statement.

"Create in me a clean heart, O God, and renew a steadfast spirit within me."
—Psalm 51:10

_____

_____

_____

DAY 5

HEART TO HEART

The Hebrew word David used in Psalm 51:10, which is translated "create," is the same word used in Genesis 1:1: *"In the beginning God created ... "* The word means to fashion, shape, or form. *"Now the earth was formless and empty, darkness was over the surface of the deep, and the Spirit of God was hovering over the waters"* (Genesis 1:2). The Holy Spirit is alluding to the beginning to define the work of God in our hearts.

Remember *gezerah shavah* (cut equally)? Let's look at a statement that will immediately take the reader back to Genesis 1:2, when the earth was formless and empty. I borrow the basis of these thoughts from a brilliant sermon by Dr. Joseph Novenson called "Decreation and Recreation."

I looked at the earth,
*   and it was formless and empty.*
—Jeremiah 4:23

Do you see the *gezerah shavah*? Formless and empty—the earth before God speaks order and light. Formless and empty—the hearts of His people when they leave the Word of God behind.

God, through Jeremiah, is reprimanding His rebellious people. He is telling them that their sin is distancing them from Him, and so is bringing into their lives the opposite of what His Word brings. When they are far from His Word, they remove themselves from what His Word provides. In Jeremiah, He is using the metaphor of the earth, but is using it to depict the empty, barren wasteland that their hearts have become. Formless and empty.

So, then, the remedy? Create, O God.

Once again, O God, hover over the emptiness that my heart has become and let there be order. Let there be life. Let there be righteousness and purity and steadfastness.

What God requires of you He provides for you. Purity comes from Him, transferring the law to the inside and being the law within you. Transforming wasteland into lush vineyard. Transforming formless emptiness into the image of His Son.

Look at the heart of Rabbi Jesus—the heart He promises to create in His disciples. What does a pure, unalloyed heart look like?

Set Apart

Sacrifice and offering you did not desire,
    but my ears you have pierced;
burnt offerings and sin offerings
    you did not require.

Then I said, "Here I am, I have come—
    it is written about me in the scroll.
I desire to do your will, O my God;
    your law is within my heart."
—Psalm 40:6–8

In the Book of Hebrews, the writer uses this quote to identify the Messiah.

Therefore, when Christ came into the world, he said:

"Sacrifice and offering you did not desire,
    but a body you prepared for me;
with burnt offerings and sin offerings
    you were not pleased.
Then I said, 'Here I am—it is
    written about me in the scroll—
I have come to do your will, O God.'"
—Hebrews 10:5–7

We read elsewhere in the Psalms: *"The law of his God is in his heart; his feet do not slip"* (Psalm 37:31).

The unalloyed, steadfast heart of Jesus, now being recreated in you, has one focus. What is it?

"My food," **said Jesus,** ***"is to do the will of him who sent me and to finish his work."***
—John 4:34

"For I have come down from heaven not to do my will but to do the will of him who sent me."
—John 6:38

When the law is written in your heart, what does it create?

_____

_____

❧ ❧ ❧

They Shall See God

The pure in heart will live in a state of blessedness, fully supplied and content, and that blessedness will be realized in seeing God. This is yet another way to say they will live in the kingdom.

To see God is not to see with the physical eyes, but with *"the eyes of your heart"* (Ephesians 1:18). Jesus used the language of seeing when He talked about how He recognized the Father's activity while He was in the form of man.

> *Jesus gave them this answer: "I tell you the truth, the Son can do nothing by himself; he can do only what he sees his Father doing, because whatever the Father does the Son also does. For the Father loves the Son and shows him all he does."*
> —John 5:19–20

Let's go back to David's Psalm 51. This psalm is probably the basis of Jesus' words about the pure in heart. Let's see what follows David's plea for God to create in him a clean heart and renew a steadfast spirit.

> *Create in me a pure heart, O God,*
> *   and renew a steadfast spirit within me.*
> *Do not cast me from your presence*
> *   or take your Holy Spirit from me.*
> —Psalm 51:10–11

David says, "Do not throw me out of Your presence—where I can see You." The word translated "presence" in Hebrew refers to the face or the countenance. Don't take your face away from me, David begged.

What did David believe would be the result of his impure heart? He would not see God. He would have to leave God's face.

Rabbi Jesus reminds the people of what the Torah had always taught them. David said it long ago. The pure in heart will know the face of God.

Blessed are the pure in heart, for they shall see God.

Set Apart

Can you purify your own heart?

_____

Since the Scripture teaches from the beginning that purification can only come with the shedding of blood, how does that translate into your life?

_____

_____

_____

What are some alloys that you find in your own heart?

_____

_____

_____

Would you place those on the altar now and let the fountain filled with blood flow in you so freely that your heart is cleansed and washed and made new?

_____

_____

_____

❧ ❧ ❧

WEEK FOUR

WEEK FIVE

DAY 1

BLESSED ARE THE PEACEMAKERS

"The fruit of righteousness will be peace; the effect of righteousness will be quietness and confidence forever" (Isaiah 32:17).

The fruit of a tree proves what kind of tree it is. Apple trees grow apples. Peach trees grow peaches. You can identify a tree by its fruit.

What is the fruit of righteousness? Peace.

Remember the Hebrew style of saying the same thing twice in different words. These two phrases are two ways of saying the same thing. *"The fruit of righteousness will be peace"* is another way of saying *"the effect of righteousness will be quietness and confidence forever."* It helps us define the words. *Fruit* is the same as *effect. Peace* means essentially the same thing as *quietness and confidence forever.*

Let's take a closer look at the words in this statement. The word translated here as *"fruit"* is a Hebrew word that means "workmanship, something created or fashioned." The word is used in the Genesis creation account to describe the work of God's hands in fashioning and forming that which He created.

When righteousness works, what does it fashion? What is its workmanship—the fruit of its labor? What is its masterpiece? Peace.

The word translated *"effect"* is a Hebrew word that usually means "work produced through servitude." A derivative of the word is used to denote the work of the priests and Levites in service to God.

When righteousness forces a result, what is it? Quietness and trust forever. Peace.

Quietness means "tranquil, undisturbed and still." *Trust* means "confident and untroubled."

Pull all the thoughts together and write out your commentary on this verse: *"The fruit of righteousness will be peace; the effect of righteousness will be quietness and confidence forever"* **(Isaiah 32:17).**

_____

_____

Rabbi Jesus declared that peacemakers would live in a state of blessedness. He was talking about people who actively worked to bring peace into relationships.

To make peace, a person must be at peace. A person who is filled with turmoil will inject that into relationships and situations. A person who is filled with peace will diffuse peace into relationships and situations.

To be a peacemaker, you have to be peaceful. But peace comes at a price.

Shalom

Shalom is the Hebrew word usually translated "peace," but our English word *peace* does not capture it very well. *Shalom* means a state of completeness, wholeness, unity, fulfillment. It refers to emotional, physical, relational, and financial well-being, and even encompasses safety.

Shalom is the state in which God wants His people to live. In His shalom, you are not promised wealth, but you are promised provision. Blessedness is a state of *shalom*. In the introduction to Sabbath rest in Genesis 2:1, the Scripture uses a Hebrew word for *finished* that means "to be completed or to have brought to perfection and fullness." The seventh day, Sabbath, is the day that all work is to be finished so that the people rest. The first Sabbath was the day on which God rested after having completed all His work. The number seven in Hebrew is the number that represents completeness and perfection. Sabbath is a day of *shalom*.

Paul writes, *"We proclaim him, admonishing and teaching everyone with all wisdom, so that we may present everyone* perfect *in Christ. To this end I labor, struggling with all his energy, which so powerfully works in me"* (Colossians 1:28–29, author's emphasis). Paul likely has in mind the Hebrew concept of completeness and fullness, of *shalom*.

To see the original *shalom* that God has always meant for His people to experience, look at creation and see how He set things up in the beginning. Eden, before sin, was the perfect illustration of *shalom*.

Peace between God and His people. Intimacy, love, trust.

His people at peace with each other. Cooperation, respect, unity.

His people in a state of inner peace and rest. No worry. No anxiety. No anger or resentment or rebellion.

The Sabbath day would become a shadow and hint of the *shalom* of Eden. All the week's work is completed. The day is given to rest and restoration. Nothing will detract from the enjoyment of fellowship with God.

Canaan, the land of rest, would be a shadow and hint of the *shalom* of Eden. Here, in the Promised Land, the buildings were already built, the crops were already planted. The abundance was provided. God intended rest from their enemies. The land was prepared for them, and they were to enjoy the land that God had given them.

The kingdom is what all the shadows of *shalom* had been leading up to. Eden, Sabbath, Canaan—all whispers of the kingdom. When you enter the kingdom, you enter *shalom*. In the kingdom, the King offers a *shalom* that begins in the heart, and radiates out to circumstances and relationships.

Looking at Eden, Sabbath, and Canaan as shadows of the peace in which God wants His people to live, what do you see in the shadows and types? What does each picture for you about the peace God wants to give you?

✄ **Eden**

_____

_____

✄ **Sabbath**

_____

_____

✄ **Canaan**

_____

_____

DAY 2

PEACE WITH GOD

"Since we have been justified through faith, we have peace with God through our Lord Jesus Christ, through whom we have gained access by faith into this grace in which we now stand."
—Romans 5:1–2

In the Old Covenant, a series of sacrifices was established, each picturing the work that Jesus would accomplish on our behalf to bring us into relationship with God, from whom our sins had estranged us. The prescribed sin offering, which brought the sinner back into fellowship with God, required the sacrifice of an unblemished animal whose blood was poured on the altar. Before the animal was killed, the worshiper pressed his hand upon the animals head and confessed his sin, symbolically laying it on the animal. The body of the animal, once the blood was shed, was taken outside the encampment and burned.

The writer of Hebrews makes clear that this blood sacrifice was a shadow of Jesus' sacrifice on the Cross.

> *The high priest carries the blood of animals into the Most Holy Place as a sin offering, but the bodies are burned outside the camp. And so Jesus also suffered outside the city gate to make the people holy through his own blood.*
> —Hebrews 13:11–12

As Paul states in Romans 5:1–2, quoted above, the peace we have with God is ours through our Lord Jesus Christ, who acted as our sin sacrifice and so brought us into relationship with the Father.

Peace with God came at a great price.

Peace Within

When Eden was disrupted by the entrance of sin, the effect was not only to bring disruption to the relationship between God and humans, but also to bring discord within the souls of humans themselves. Peace was no longer the state of the human's soul. Instead, chaos began to reign. Anxiety, fear, anger, envy, lust…all invaded the human soul. Man was made for holiness, and sin brings disorder. Lost and searching for their moorings, humans apart from God are unsettled, formless, and void, longing for something they can't even name. When Christ comes to indwell a restless soul, the peace of Christ takes up residence.

Paul describes the process this way:

Those who live according to the sinful nature have their minds set on what that nature desires; but those who live in accordance with the Spirit have their minds set on what the Spirit desires. The mind of sinful man is death, but the mind controlled by the Spirit is life and peace; the sinful mind is hostile to God. It does not submit to God's law, nor can it do so. Those controlled by the sinful nature cannot please God. You, however, are controlled not by the sinful nature but by the Spirit, if the Spirit of God lives in you.
—Romans 8:5–9

Peace Between

For God was pleased to have all his fullness dwell in him, and through him to reconcile to himself all things, whether things on earth or things in heaven, by making peace through his blood, shed on the cross.

Once you were alienated from God and were enemies in your minds because of your evil behavior. But now he has reconciled you by Christ's physical body through death to present you holy in his sight, without blemish and free from accusation.
—Colossians 1:19–22

Paul may well have been thinking about the peace offering of the sacrificial system when he penned these words, and alluding to it, knowing many in his audience would also pick up on the symbolism. Most rabbis, including Jesus, made heavy use of symbolism, allusion, and metaphor. Paul used the same style of teaching, one with which his Jewish audiences were familiar.

The peace offering was one of the blood sacrifices of the Old Testament. The purpose of the peace offering was not to make peace with God, but to celebrate the peace with God that had been established through the sin offering.

In the peace offering, the animal was slain at the tabernacle door and the priest sprinkled the blood on the altar. Then the animal was offered on the altar as a whole burnt offering, a pleasing aroma to the Lord. The person offering the sacrifice and the priest and the priest's children all ate the meat of the sacrifice. The aroma of the whole burnt offering rose before the Lord, making God part of the meal.

The suggested symbolism was that all were consuming the body of the same sacrifice, and so partaking of one flesh, and so becoming one. Peace between God and the one offering the sacrifice, and between those consuming the sacrifice. All being unified through the flesh offered on the altar.

Set Apart

Reconciled to God and to each other through the Peace Offering. We become one with Him and so one with each other through Him.

For he himself is our peace, *who has made the two one and has destroyed the barrier, the dividing wall of hostility, by abolishing in his flesh the law with its commandments and regulations. His purpose was to create in himself one new man out of the two, thus making peace, and in this one body to reconcile both of them to God through the cross, by which he put to death their hostility. He came and preached peace to you who were far away and peace to those who were near. For through him we both have access to the Father by one Spirit.*
—Ephesians 2:14–18 (author's emphasis)

He will stand and shepherd his flock
    in the strength of the LORD,
    in the majesty of the name of the LORD *his God.*
And they will live securely,
     for then his greatness will reach to the ends of the earth.
    And he will be their peace.
—Micah 5:4–5 (author's emphasis)

Peacemakers

Only those who have experienced peace can make peace. King Jesus says that His kingdom is made up of peacemakers. The peace that He has brought us has come at great cost. The peace we will diffuse will come at cost to us. Peace is never cheap.

Look at the following Scriptures and determine what it will cost you to be a peacemaker.

Therefore, as God's chosen people, holy and dearly loved, clothe your-selves with compassion, kindness, humility, gentleness and patience. Bear with each other and forgive whatever grievances you may have against one another. Forgive as the Lord forgave you. And over all these virtues put on love, which binds them all together in perfect unity.

    Let the peace of Christ rule in your hearts, since as members of one body you were called to peace.
—**Colossians 3:12–15**

Let us therefore make every effort to do what leads to peace and to mutual edification.
—Romans 14:19

Bless those who persecute you; bless and do not curse. Rejoice with those who rejoice, and weep with those who weep.

Be of the same mind toward one another; do not be haughty in mind, but associate with the lowly. Do not be wise in your own estimation.

Never pay back evil for evil to anyone. Respect what is right in the sight of all men.

If possible, so far as it depends on you, be at peace with all men.

Never take your own revenge, beloved, but leave room for the wrath of God, for it is written: "VENGEANCE IS MINE, I WILL REPAY," says the Lord.

"BUT IF YOUR ENEMY IS HUNGRY, FEED HIM, AND IF HE IS THIRSTY, GIVE HIM A DRINK; FOR IN SO DOING YOU WILL HEAP BURNING COALS ON HIS HEAD."

Do not be overcome by evil, but overcome evil with good.
—Romans 12:14–21

As you let the Spirit speak to you through His Word about being a peacemaker, what is He saying to you about your current situation? Write it out.

_____

_____

_____

_____

WEEK FIVE

DAY 3
OUTRAGEOUS PEACEMAKING

How did Jesus expound on the kind of peacemaking that will mark the daily rhythms of the kingdom? He didn't talk about just keeping your cool, or appeasing the angry person, or being accommodating. No, He called for outrageous acts of peacemaking.

"You have heard that the ancients were told, 'YOU SHALL NOT COMMIT MURDER' and 'Whoever commits murder shall be liable to the court.'

"But I say to you that everyone who is angry with his brother shall be guilty before the court; and whoever says to his brother, 'You good-for-nothing,' shall be guilty before the supreme court; and whoever says, 'You fool,' shall be guilty enough to go into the fiery hell.

"Therefore if you are presenting your offering at the altar, and there remember that your brother has something against you, leaving your offering there before the altar and go; first be reconciled to your brother, and then come and present your offering.

"Make friends quickly with your opponent at law while you are with him on the way, so that your opponent may not hand you over to the judge, and the judge to the officer, and you be thrown into prison.

"Truly I say to you, you will not come out of there until you have paid up to the last cent.

"You have heard that it was said, 'YOU SHALL NOT COMMIT ADULTERY'; but I say to you that everyone who looks at a woman with lust for her has already committed adultery with her in his heart.

"If your right eye makes you stumble, tear it out and throw it from you; for it is better for you to lose one of the parts of your body, than for your whole body to be thrown into hell.

"If your right hand makes you stumble, cut it off and throw it from you; for it is better for you to lose one of the parts of your body, than for your whole body to go into hell.

"It was said, 'WHOEVER SENDS HIS WIFE AWAY, LET HIM GIVE HER A CERTIFICATE OF DIVORCE'; but I say to you that everyone who divorces his wife, except for the reason of unchastity, makes her commit adultery; and whoever marries a divorced woman commits adultery.

"Again, you have heard that the ancients were told, 'YOU SHALL NOT MAKE FALSE VOWS, BUT SHALL FULFILL YOUR VOWS TO THE LORD.'

"But I say to you , make no oath at all, either by heaven, for it is the throne of God, or by the earth, for it is the footstool of His feet, or by Jerusalem, for it is THE CITY OF THE GREAT KING.

"Nor shall you make an oath by your head, for you cannot make one hair white or black.

"But let your statement be, 'Yes, yes' or 'No, no'; anything beyond these is of evil.

"You have heard that it was said, 'AN EYE FOR AN EYE, AND A TOOTH FOR A TOOTH.'

"But I say to you, do not resist an evil person; but whoever slaps you on your right cheek, turn the other to him also.

"If anyone wants to sue you and take your shirt, let him have your coat also.

"Whoever forces you to go one mile, go with him two.

"Give to him who asks of you, and do not turn away from him who wants to borrow from you.

"You have heard that it was said, 'YOU SHALL LOVE YOUR NEIGHBOR and hate your enemy.'

"But I say to you, love your enemies and pray for those who persecute you, so that you may be sons of your Father who is in heaven; for He causes His sun to rise on the evil and the good, and sends rain on the righteous and the unrighteous.

"For if you love those who love you, what reward do you have? Do not even the tax collectors do the same?

"If you greet only your brothers, what more are you doing than others? Do not even the Gentiles do the same?

"Therefore you are to be perfect, as your heavenly Father is perfect."
—Matthew 5:21–48 (NASB)

Jesus gave a series of instructions, each framed in real-life settings. He used cultural references that were familiar to His audience, but that contained eternal truths, which can relate to any culture at any time. He was describing how a peacemaker would live, every day surrounded by humans with human failings and challenging circumstances. The call to live in the kingdom is not a call to live in a bubble. It is a call to live in the nitty-gritty, rubber-meets-the-road reality of planet earth.

Jesus clearly did not list every single possible scenario in which His disciples are to act in ways contrary to the ways of the world. His intention is not to lay out a new law for every potential situation. These statements follow immediately His declaration that He has come to fulfill the law, not to abolish it, and that His disciples must have a righteousness that exceeds that of the scribes and Pharisees. (Review Matthew 5:17–20).

Starting in verse 21, Jesus begins to list examples of how one's righteousness would exceed the righteousness of the religious leaders. As we look at these instructions on how to live in ways that will make peace, even in contentious settings, look for a principle that these situations illustrate.

In each case, He is saying that the law goes beyond behavior. The law deals with the heart. Jesus makes demands that are impossible to obey. He is talking to an audience that is more accustomed to discussing behavioral rules than heart conditions. "Give me a rule to follow so I can be righteous! Give me a law to obey that will bring me eternal life!" is the more typical expectation.

Jesus is doing what He has been doing from the beginning of the sermon. He is laying out a law that cannot be kept from the outside, but can only be obeyed by Jesus living in you, transforming your heart, imparting His power and life.

How would you define a principle that runs through each of these situations and would also carry over into any situation?

_____

_____

_____

_____

Jesus takes it to the heart. When the law is filled to its fullness, then actions that don't have heart obedience behind them don't make the grade. Man looks at the outward appearance, but the Lord looks at the heart.

In kingdom peacemaking, the disciple takes the initiative. The disciple lays aside pride, risks rejection or ridicule. Peace, Jesus indicates, is more than absence of conflict. Peace is not passive. For example, if a person with the authority to do so, ordered you to go with him one mile, then going with him one mile would avoid conflict. But Jesus tells us to _make_ peace. Create something out of nothing. Don't be satisfied with keeping things on even keel. Make peace.

In order to go that second mile, the peace has to be in you. It is a peace that has grown out of meekness. A strong, settled, contented person, anchored to eternity's realities, has the courage and the boldness to be outrageous in making peace. *"The fruit of righteousness will be peace; the effect of righteousness will be quietness and confidence forever"* (Isaiah 32:17).

Peacebusters

Where do conflicts come from? Let's look at James 4:1–3. James is specifically referring to conflicts among believers, but the principles he lays out would account for most, if not all, conflicts between people.

> *What causes fights and quarrels among you? Don't they come from your desires that battle within you? You want something but don't get it. You kill and covet, but you cannot have what you want. You quarrel and fight. You do not have, because you do not ask God. When you ask, you do not receive, because you ask with wrong motives, that you may spend what you get on your pleasures.*
> —James 4:1–3

What causes fights and quarrels among you?

1. *They come from your desires that battle within you.* A heart that is not at peace is not able to diffuse peace into situations. Your inner conflicts will spill over into conflict with others.

Paul says a similar thing to the Galatians.

> *You, my brothers, were called to be free. But do not use your freedom to indulge the sinful nature; rather, serve one another in love. The entire law is summed up in a single command: "Love your neighbor as yourself." If you keep on biting and devouring each other, watch out or you will be destroyed by each other.*
>
> *So I say, live by the Spirit, and you will not gratify the desires of the sinful nature. For the sinful nature desires what is contrary to the Spirit, and the Spirit what is contrary to the sinful nature. They are in conflict with each other, so that you do not do what you want.*
> —Galatians 5:13–17

2. *You want something but don't get it.* You have inner conflict because you want something—something external—and you don't get it. You are focusing on outward circumstances instead of keeping your focus on the kingdom.

3. *You kill and covet, but you cannot have what you want. You quarrel and*

fight. James is not necessarily talking about physical murder, but the kinds of inner thoughts and attitudes that are the basis of murder. You are trying to get what you want from one another. You are expecting someone else to be or do or provide what you think you desire. No one can provide what you desire except God. You quarrel and fight and blame each other and accuse each other.

4. *You do not have, because you do not ask God.* You are looking to others to provide what only God can. You are looking outward when you should be looking Godward.

5. *When you ask, you do not receive, because you ask with wrong motives, that you may spend what you get on your pleasures.* When you finally get around to asking God, you are asking God for what you think you need—for what you have been trying to get out of others. You have *desires* that battle within you, and now you want God to give you what you want so you can satisfy those very *desires.* In Greek, the two words are the same—earlier translated *desires* and here translated *pleasures.*

Consider any conflict you are dealing with. Is the conflict first based in your heart? What relationship in your life is causing you distress?

_____

_____

Is someone treating you unfairly in your judgment? Are you being taken for granted?

_____

_____

It could be that your actions and responses are aggressive and hostile. If so, do you create more discord and raise the level of the disagreement? Are you setting up a situation where there is a "winner" and a "loser"? Do you see that attitude ratchets up the hostility?

_____

It could be that your actions are passive, but inside you are seething. Are your actions avoiding a confrontation, but inside your anger is growing and coming out in ways that may not even be part of the situation?

_____

_____

What is the Lord saying to you about how to be an outrageous peacemaker in your situation? What does it cost you?

_____

_____

_____

_____

Peace comes from inside and spreads to those around you. Jesus listed several representative situations that bring contention and instructed His disciples how to handle those potentially explosive situations and be aggressive peacemakers. Take a situation in which conflict is a given, and make peace.

Make peace. Peace isn't there until you make it. Create it. Bring peace out of chaos and disorder. Be like your Father.

DAY 4
THEY WILL BE CALLED SONS OF GOD

"Blessed are the peacemakers, for they will be called sons of God" (Matthew 5:9).

Here the Greek word translated "sons" is the word for masculine offspring. Don't worry. Women are not excluded. To be called a daughter in that ancient society would have little clout. But to be called a son—now that had heft. A son was the heir and the name-bearer. The son was to carry on the work of the father. The son was the exact replica of the father. Rabbi Jesus says to both men and women—you will be called sons.

They will be *called* sons of God. The word has many meanings. One is the obvious meaning that peacemakers will be known as sons of God. But let's add some other layers, each legitimate inferences in the context and from the word used. It can mean "to invite or to call to oneself." It is also the word used for the call of God—the appointment. It can refer to a summons. It can mean "to call out loud—to call to."

> *God, who calls you into his kingdom and glory.*
> —1 Thessalonians 2:12

> *God, who has called you into fellowship with his Son Jesus Christ our Lord, is faithful.*
> —1 Corinthians 1:9

> *And you also are among those who are called to belong to Jesus Christ.*
> —Romans 1:6

Radical, outrageous peacemakers are known as sons of God. People who observe them can't help but notice the likeness. God has invited them to Himself, called them out to set them apart. God has summoned them and called out loud. "Son! You are a peacemaker!"

> *How great is the love the Father has lavished on us, that we should be called children of God! And that is what we are!*
> —1 John 3:1

Day 4: They Will Be Called Sons of God 139

My Father's Son

The peacemakers are like their Father in several ways. First, they reach out to make peace at cost to themselves. When the Father made peace with us, He did it like this:

> *You see, at just the right time, when we were still powerless, Christ died for the ungodly. Very rarely will anyone die for a righteous man, though for a good man someone might possibly dare to die. But God demonstrates his own love for us in this: While we were still sinners, Christ died for us.*
> —Romans 5:6–8

Second, they *make* peace. They create peace from scratch. When the situation is empty and formless, they turn it into peace.

> *In the beginning God created the heavens and the earth. Now the earth was formless and empty, darkness was over the surface of the deep, and the Spirit of God was hovering over the waters. And God said, "Let there be light," and there was light.*
> —Genesis 1:1–3

Third, they find pleasure in creating peace where chaos had been. They know there is *"joy for those who promote peace"* (Proverbs 12:20).

> *God saw all that he had made, and it was very good.*
> —Genesis 1:31

Only having the Son living presently in your heart will you have the inclination or the power to create peace. Apart from Him, our hearts would never be willing to let go of pride and self-interest so that we can make peace.

> *You received the Spirit of sonship. And by him we cry, "Abba, Father." The Spirit himself testifies with our spirit that we are God's children. Now if we are children, then we are heirs—heirs of God and co-heirs with Christ, if indeed we share in his sufferings in order that we may also share in his glory.*
> —Romans 8:15–17

> *Because you are sons, God sent the Spirit of his Son into our hearts, the Spirit who calls out, "Abba, Father."*
> —Galatians 4:6–7

In your own words, what does Jesus mean by "peacemaker"?

_____

_____

How does righteousness produce peace?

_____

_____

Why is a peacemaker known as a son of God?

_____

_____

DAY 5

BLESSED ARE THOSE WHO ARE PERSECUTED BECAUSE OF RIGHTEOUSNESS

Those who suffer persecution because of their righteousness live in a state of blessedness. Notice, this does not include those who are disliked because of their self-righteousness, or because of their condescending attitude, or because of their hypercritical, judgmental approach. It does not include those who are unwelcome because of their religious demeanor.

This beatitude has many implications. For the purposes of this study, we will focus on one direction. I don't want to seem to gloss over the kind of physical persecution that Christians have suffered and are now suffering for the sake of the gospel. Most of us will not know those experiences. I would be incapable of doing justice to a subject so holy and so outside the scope of my life experiences. How precious in the Lord's sight are the sufferings His dear ones endure for His name's sake. History is filled with these heroes, known and unknown. At this moment, all over the globe, Christians are suffering in physical ways because of their devotion to Christ. Many choose to put themselves in situations where their faith will make them targets, all for the sake of the gospel. How blessed are these courageous believers; their welfare should be a topic of our fervent prayers. However, this beatitude has other implications—some that will be more in line with what you and I are experiencing on a daily basis. I think this focus would lend itself best to this study.

Let's look at how *The Message* translates this passage:

You're blessed when your commitment to God provokes persecution. The persecution drives you even deeper into God's kingdom.

Not only that—count yourselves blessed every time people put you down or throw you out or speak lies about you to discredit me. What it means is that the truth is too close for comfort and they are uncomfortable. You can be glad when that happens—give a cheer, even!—for though they don't like it, I do! And all heaven applauds. And know that you are in good company. My prophets and witnesses have always gotten into this kind of trouble.
—Matthew 5:10–12 (*The Message*)

Persecution Lite

What kinds of persecution do most of us endure from the people around us? Do people sometimes belittle my beliefs and try to make me feel silly? Who cares! Do people perhaps talk behind my back about my fanaticism? So what! Do some people try to discredit me? Big deal! Do secular media or other secular institutions mock my beliefs? Who cares! May I be honest? I just can't come up with any real persecution that I experience from people. Yet the Scripture makes this statement: *"In fact, everyone who wants to live a godly life in Christ Jesus will be persecuted"* (2 Timothy 3:12).

I can't claim persecution from people, but my fight is not against flesh and blood.

War of the Worlds

The word translated "persecuted," both the Greek word and the Hebrew word Jesus would likely have used, means "to be pursued." Who might be pursuing me? *"Your enemy the devil prowls around like a roaring lion looking for someone to devour"* (1 Peter 5:8–9).

Read the following Scripture, then answer the questions below.

Be self-controlled and alert. Your enemy the devil prowls around like a roaring lion looking for someone to devour. Resist him, standing firm in the faith, because you know that your brothers throughout the world are undergoing the same kind of sufferings.

And the God of all grace, who called you to his eternal glory in Christ, after you have suffered a little while, will himself restore you and make you strong, firm and steadfast. To him be the power for ever and ever. Amen.
—1 Peter 5:8–11

How might your enemy in the spiritual realm be compared to a roaring lion looking for someone to devour?

_____

_____

Does Peter consider this suffering?

_____

Why will God restore you "after you have suffered a little while"? Why not immediately?

_____

_____

Can God make any redemptive use of Satan's schemes?

_____

_____

We have an enemy, an adversary in the spiritual realm. He is real. He is alert and watching for every opportunity to pursue us. His goal, now that he has lost us for eternity, is to keep us from the fullness of what Jesus has for us now. He has only one weapon—a weapon he wields with great skill. Lies. *"When he lies, he speaks his native language, for he is a liar and the father of lies"* (John 8:44).

Your enemy never ever tells the truth, *"for there is no truth in him"* (John 8:44). Yet he is so skilled at using lies that when he lies, it sounds like truth.

Your enemy hates you and has only one goal in his dealings with you: to steal, kill, and destroy anything that God has established in your life. The more you learn to live the surrendered life that Jesus describes in His inaugural address, the more your enemy will pursue you.

Nothing to fear here. Your enemy has a very limited reach into your life. In fact, he has no reach at all unless it is allowed by your Father. And your Father will allow no access to you except that which ultimately will be turned against the enemy and will accrue to your benefit.

The Battle Plan

Just like the Father uses people, relationships, and circumstances in your life to train you in the ways of the kingdom and to force your faith out of hiding, your enemy seeks to make use of those same people, relationships, and circumstances. Every situation that your enemy means to use against you, God means to use for your benefit.

Under God's authority, your enemy can only bring difficulties into your life that have passed through the sieve of the Father's great love for you and from which all the destructive force has been strained. What gets through is to be used for your good only.

Your enemy is on the lookout for the very places where your flesh is vulnerable. Soul wounds not quite healed. Areas where you are still trying to accomplish your own holiness—not surrendered to the indwelling power of Christ.

As we look for a moment at the enemy's battle plan, remember that, although he uses people, relationships, and circumstances, your only enemy is in the spiritual realm. *"For our struggle is not against flesh and blood, but against the rulers, against the authorities, against the powers of this dark world and against the spiritual forces of evil in the heavenly realms"* (Ephesians 6:12).

When Satan uses people, that does not mean that the person is evil or is cooperating with Satan. Rather, it means that Satan sees how that person's personality, or the words he speaks to you, or some imagined slight could be used to activate your weakness. So, a person who speaks words meant only kindly uses a tone of voice or a gesture that subconsciously reminds you of your mother, from whom you received much harsh criticism. Now, Satan's forces begin to lie to you. You don't recognize that it is Satan's forces. He doesn't announce himself. No, to you it feels like your own thoughts reasoning and making a rational summation. "She thinks you are not good enough. She thinks you have done everything wrong. She means to hurt your feelings. And you have done everything wrong, like you always do. You should stop trying. But first, you should say something to her to let her know she's not perfect either!"

Your enemy is persecuting you. Saying all manner of evil against you falsely. Working to divide you from another member of the body. Now, consider this. If the enemy is like a roaring lion looking for someone to devour, how does a lion get his prey in position? He isolates his prey from the herd. Cuts her off. Gets her alone. Do you see the process?

Let's say that something unexpected and challenging comes into your experience. You lose your job, let's say. Now Satan's forces take advantage of the situation to prod your inclination to fear. "If God were really looking after you, this would not happen. God is not dependable. And, besides, you are so terrible and worthless that God would not waste His time looking after you. You deserve to fail." Do you see?

Now redefine what is happening to you. Your enemy is telling lies, but they sound true. His lies are designed brilliantly so that they magnify your own thoughts. He is persecuting you.

Blessed are you!

If your enemy were not feeling threatened by you, he would not work to distract you. The very incidents that he wants to use to weaken you, God wants to use to strengthen you. Your enemy's clever manipulation only serves to identify places where your flesh is still active. This is to your advantage if you deliberately resist the lie and identify with the truth. When you do that, the flesh your enemy is able to target is surrendered to the life of Christ in you and when the enemy thinks he is taking on your flesh, he finds himself confronting Jesus Himself. Who's the loser now?

Are there any areas in your life right now where you are experiencing the persecution of your spiritual enemy?

_____

_____

How are you redefining the situation right now?

_____

_____

How can you live in a state of blessedness while you are undergoing this persecution?

_____

_____

Theirs Is the Kingdom

Full circle. The first beatitude proclaims *"theirs is the kingdom,"* and the last beatitude proclaims *"theirs is the kingdom."* All the Beatitudes between said the same thing in different words. Jesus introduced multiple ways to describe the kingdom.

Jesus introduced His public ministry by describing the heart that would produce holy behavior. He was defining His own heart, which He would be recreating in His disciples as they let Him live in them and through them. He announced that He was bringing the law into its fullness and that the law would not change in content but in location. The law, which had been on the outside—commanding—would now be on the inside—promising. Those set apart for God's purposes would be made holy both in nature and in behavior.

Before we move to the final week of this study, take some time to review and to solidify what you have learned. How would you explain or define the following?

- **Blessed**

_____

_____

- **Poor in spirit**

_____

_____

- **Meek**

_____

_____

- **Mourning**

_____

_____

- **Hungry and thirsty for righteousness**

_____

_____

❧ **Merciful**

_____

_____

❧ **Pure in heart**

_____

_____

❧ **Peacemaker**

_____

_____

❧ **Persecuted**

_____

_____

❧ ❧ ❧

WEEK SIX

DAY 1

THE HEART OF PRAYER

In the Sermon on the Mount, Rabbi Jesus outlined prayer. Like the Beatitudes themselves, and many of the sayings in the sermon, this prayer outline reflects Jesus's immersion in the Hebrew Scriptures and the Talmud, or oral law. The Jewish people have a prayer called the *Amidah*. This, during Jesus' day, was a series of 18 petitions and benedictions. It was prayed by devout Jews at least once daily, and was included in the daily Temple liturgy. The word *amidah* means "standing" because the prayer was to be spoken standing. Jesus, you can be sure, had prayed the *Amidah* hundreds of times. The *Amidah* has a form very similar to the Lord's Prayer that Jesus taught His disciples.

A condensed form of the prayer was also allowed. It was common for a rabbi to teach his disciples his own version of the *Amidah*. He would teach his disciples what he considered the heart of the prayer. Notice in Luke's account that Jesus's disciples asked Him to teach them to pray *"as John taught his disciples"* (Luke 11:1).

The prayer that Jesus taught His disciples was in response to their direct request, *"Lord, teach us to pray"* (Luke 11:1). Their request followed immediately after one of Jesus's own extended times of prayer. They wanted to know how to pray like Jesus prayed. They didn't want just another set of words to say. They wanted to know how to pray like their rabbi prayed. Jesus answered them with what we call the Lord's Prayer.

This same prayer is included in His inaugural address. This was one of the introductory lessons Jesus wanted to communicate to set the tone for His ministry. In essence, Jesus said, "This is how I pray." Nothing is more revealing of the heart than prayer. Rabbi Jesus—King Jesus—shows us the landscape of the heart set apart. His prayer reveals the heart that the Beatitudes have described.

The whole sermon is focused on taking the rituals of religion into the heart. Though many would have prayed the *Amidah* as it was supposed to be prayed—with heartfelt urgency—others had let it become a show meant to put them center stage.

"And when you pray, do not be like the hypocrites, for they love to pray standing in the synagogues and on the street corners to be seen by men. I tell you the truth, they have received their reward in full. But when you pray, go into your room, close the door and pray to your Father, who is unseen. Then your Father, who sees what is done in secret, will reward you. And when you pray, do not keep on babbling like pagans, for they think they will be heard because of their many words. Do not be like them, for your Father knows what you need before you ask him.
"This, then, is how you should pray:
"'Our Father in heaven,
hallowed be your name,
your kingdom come,
your will be done
on earth as it is in heaven.
Give us today our daily bread.
Forgive us our debts,
as we also have forgiven our debtors.
And lead us not into temptation,
but deliver us from the evil one.'"
—Matthew 6:5–13

This week, let's examine the prayer that Jesus taught His disciples to pray because it is how He prayed. It is the prayer of the heart set apart.

Our Father

"Our Father in heaven, hallowed be your name" (Matthew 6:9).

One of the most surprising truths that Jesus revealed about God is that we can call Him Father. This offended the religious leaders of His day. *"For this reason the Jews tried all the harder to kill him; not only was he breaking the Sabbath, but he was even calling God his own Father, making himself equal with God"* (John 5:18). That made God too accessible.

The idea of God as Father was not foreign to Jewish thinking. The Old Testament hints at His father-relationship with His people, but it lacked the intimacy that Jesus gave it. Rabbi Jesus's preferred name for God was Father—Abba, Daddy, Papa. When He taught His disciples to pray like He prayed, the first lesson was, our Father. When "our Father" is the headline, then the requests that follow are all defined by the intimate, loving, safe relationship of a father to His child. In *With Christ in the School of Prayer*, Andrew Murray wrote, "It is in prayer and its answer that the interchange of love between the Father and His child takes place."

In *Live a Praying Life*, I illustrated how the relationship changes the conversation as follows:

> The intimacy and trust that grows during the process of prayer is what gives us boldness in prayer. It is the relationship of child to father that makes our words prayer. Suppose that you ordered a meal at a restaurant. When the server brought your meal, suppose she said, "That looks delicious! I think I'll try a bite." Suppose that she then took a fork and tasted your food. You'd be outraged. You would demand to see the manager. You would insist that the food be taken back.
>
> Suppose, however, that you went to a restaurant with your child. When your meal was served, imagine that your child said, "That looks delicious! I think I'll try a bite." When your child took a bite of your meal, you would not be the least bit upset. This would be a normal exchange between a child and parent.
>
> The difference between the two scenarios is not the words, or even the intent, but the relationship. The parent-child relationship gives boldness and intimacy not available to nonfamily members. The same words take on new meaning in the context of the relationship.
>
> Think of conversations and behaviors that are appropriate in the intimacy of family relationships but are too intimate and bold for less binding relationships. Consider how much freedom and access relationship gives you. As you pray, be aware of how uninhibited and audacious you are allowed to be because you are coming to your Father, not to a distant, unrelated deity.

Relationship changes the way we communicate. Long intimacy, shared history, entwined lives—this kind of relationship colors conversation. For example, I have two sisters. When I am talking to either of them, one of us might say one word or one phrase that sends us into gales of laughter. To an outsider listening in, it would seem that nothing funny had been said. However, because of our long history, a word between us says volumes.

As you live in intimacy with God, you will find the same thing playing out. A mere word may be all the prayer you need to voice in some circumstances. That one word speaks it all. As intimacy grows, the saying of prayer, in many circumstances, becomes simpler.

The kind of intimacy that results in verbal shorthand between you has at its core prolonged, intense interaction. Because of the time invested in intimate communion, an easy and loving familiarity develops. The relationship deepens through focused and deliberate time with Him, then flows naturally through the circumstances of life with an uncontrived delight in each other's company.

The Gospels give us glimpses into the kind of love the Father has for His children. Let's look at one tender moment when Jesus demonstrated the fatherhood of God. The love of a father for his child is focused and specific, not generic or general. The tiniest, weakest cry falls upon a father's ears like a clarion call. You, child of your Father, are never lost in the crowd.

A Daddy's Love

Recall the story of a nameless woman who suffered from an undiagnosed illness, tucked into the gospel of Mark, wedged into the story of a high-profile healing. Find it in Mark 5:21–43.

We only have a snapshot of her. She appears on the scene briefly. We know one fact about her: she had been hemorrhaging for 12 years. Because of the ritual impurity her condition entailed, we know that for 12 years, no one has touched her. If a man had brushed up against her, he would have been made unclean because of her impurity. Imagine the times over the last 12 years that she had accidentally defiled a man. Imagine her humiliation and shame as the man scolded her and demeaned her. He would have had to rush home, tear off his defiled clothes, and cleanse himself in elaborate ceremony. It was very inconvenient to be touched by this impure one. Surely she had learned to hide herself even in crowds. Surely she had learned to gather her garments in closely, to cover her face, to become invisible.

WEEK SIX

Before we look at her story, notice how her story is framed. The framing of a picture brings out the details, focuses the eye. Look how her story is framed: it is framed by the story of Jairus.

Jairus, a leader in the synagogue—an important man, a man of influence—burst through the crowd that mobbed Jesus and, tossing aside all pride and dignity, threw himself at Jesus's feet. No doubt the crowd parted for such an esteemed man as Jairus. "Look! Here comes Jairus! Make a way for Jairus!" they might have said. No doubt they stared as he humbled himself and begged the Teacher, "My little daughter is dying. Please come and put your hands on her so that she will be healed and live" (Mark 5:23). Jairus was a daddy, and his little daughter was dying.

If you're a daddy, and your little daughter is dying, then no price is too high, no sacrifice too great. You'll do anything. You'll forget all your pride and position. You'll ignore every other duty.

If you're a daddy, and your little daughter is dying.

The crowd followed as Jesus headed for Jairus's house. They were not a quiet, sedate crowd. They were calling His name and reaching out to grab hold of Him; talking and shouting and clamoring for His attention. As they moved in the direction of Jairus's little daughter, I imagine that the crowd grew as the word went out, "Jairus's little daughter is dying! Rabbi Jesus is going to her! Come along!"

A woman stood on the fringes, watching. Alone. *Unclean*. Her uncleanness might rub off on anyone she came in contact with and that person would be forced to go through a time-consuming cleansing ritual to wash away her touch.

She had learned to be careful in public, avoiding brushing up against another person. But a thought kept worming its way into her imagination. "If I could just touch the hem of His garment, I would be made well." The thought grew stronger until, in a moment of reckless hope, she began to work her way through the crowd. The crowd didn't part for her as it had for Jairus. She prayed not to be noticed because to be noticed was to be rejected and humiliated.

Suddenly she was close enough to reach out and touch His hem and she was flooded with His power. Her touch didn't make Him unclean; instead His touch made her clean. She felt the cleansing, healing power of His touch transform her from death to life. Joy! Celebration!

Then, to her dismay, He stopped dead in His tracks. Brought the whole crowd to a screeching halt. "Who touched Me?" He demanded. She tried to hide, tried to disappear into the crowd, but He wouldn't stop asking, "Who touched Me?"

The crowd and the disciples were agitated. Why would He stop? He was on His way to do an important job. Didn't He remember Jairus's agonized cry: "Jesus, my little daughter's dying!"

Day 1: The Heart of Prayer

There had been no daddy to part the crowds for the woman with the issue of blood; no daddy to cry out on her behalf; no daddy whose heart was breaking for her pain.

Or was there?

When at last, trembling in fear, she confessed that it was she who had touched Him, He looked into her eyes and said, "Daughter!"

Maybe, then, it wasn't just her touch that stopped Jesus in His tracks. Maybe it wasn't just her touch that caught His attention. Maybe it was the voice of her Daddy whispering, "Jesus, My little daughter's dying."

She had braced herself for the scorn she knew was coming. And found instead that He looked her in the eyes and called her by a new name: "Daughter, *your faith has healed you. Go in peace and be freed from your suffering*" (Mark 5:34, author's emphasis).

Jesus was not satisfied just to heal her body. He wanted to heal her soul. When the healing flooded her body, she had what she desired from Him. But He did not have what He desired from her. He longed to bring her into His presence where He could shower her with love. He wanted to make her whole. He wanted her to know she had a Daddy.

Now My Papa's Coming

Oswald Chambers wrote in his book *Christian Disciplines*:

> A dear little friend of mine, not four years old, facing one day some big difficulty to her little heart, with a very wise shake of her head, said, "I'll go and tell my papa." Presently she came back, this time with every fiber of her little body strutting with the pride that shone in her eye, "Now my papa's coming!" Presently her papa came, she clasped her little hands and screamed with delight, and danced round about him, unspeakably confident in her papa. Child of God, does something face you that terrifies your heart? Say, "I'll tell my Father." Then come back 'boasting' in the Lord, "Now my Father's coming." And when He comes, you too will clasp your hands in rapture, your mouth will be filled with laughter, and you will be like one that dreams.

Practice calling God "Daddy." What does it mean in your circumstances right now that He is your Papa?

_____

_____

_____

_____

Fatherhood

In the Hebraic mind, the concept of God's fatherhood was tied to the creation account. As God created the earth and established life upon it, He pronounced that each species would bring forth its own kind.

> *And God said, "Let the land produce living creatures according to their kinds: livestock, creatures that move along the ground, and wild animals, each according to its kind." And it was so. God made the wild animals according to their kinds, the livestock according to their kinds, and all the creatures that move along the ground according to their kinds. And God saw that it was good.*
>
> *Then God said, "Let us make man in our image, in our likeness...."*
> *So God created man in his own image, in the image of God he created him; male and female he created them.*
> —Genesis 1:24–27

So, humankind was made in God's image, or after His kind. He "fathered" us. Later, the Lord intensified His relationship with Israel by singling them out, forming a nation that was uniquely His own. A people set apart. Through Abraham and Sarah, He fathered a nation and established a people who would display His glory, as a child displays the characteristics of the father. Through the prophet Isaiah, He described His people as *"everyone who is called by my name, whom I created for my glory, whom I formed and made"* (Isaiah 43:7). Since the Lord "formed and made" them—since they were His creation and His expression of Himself—they were as clay in His hands. They were a work in progress. *"Yet, O LORD, you are our Father. We are the clay, you are the potter; we are all the work of your hand"* (Isaiah 64:8).

Their Father was also their designer. He alone could mold them into His image. These two images, father and potter, were not incompatible: a father's responsibility is to help mold and shape the character of his children. Children can be an expression of the father both genetically and in character. Jesus, in teaching us to call God "Father," had these concepts in mind. You have been born again. God is your Father.

> *To all who received him, to those who believed in his name, he gave the right to become children of God—children born not of natural descent, nor of human decision or a husband's will, but born of God.*
> —John 1:12–13

> *For you have been born again, not of perishable seed, but of imperishable.*
> —1 Peter 1:23

> *No one who is born of God will continue to sin, because God's seed remains in him; he cannot go on sinning, because he has been born of God.*
> —1 John 3:9

As your Father, God's life is in you. He has breathed into you His breath. Just as God breathed His life into Adam at creation, so at rebirth, Jesus breathed on His disciples. *"He breathed on them and said, 'Receive the Holy Spirit'"* (John 20:22). When the Holy Spirit came at Pentecost to fill all believers, His coming sounded like a rushing wind. *"Suddenly a sound like the blowing of a violent wind came from heaven and filled the whole house where they were sitting"* (Acts 2:2). In both the Greek and Hebrew languages, the word for "spirit," "wind," and "breath" is the same. In Greek the word is *pneuma*; in Hebrew the word is *ruach*. It is fully in line with the Scripture to believe that what sounded like a mighty wind was the very breath of Jesus, breathing His life into His followers. At your rebirth, He breathed His life into you too.

Now your Father is forming you into the image of His Son, who is the image of God. He is molding you from the inside out. You are a work in progress. Listen to what I believe the Lord would want to say to you:

"Work of My Hands, I know that sometimes My sculpting hurts. Sometimes you feel as though you are looking less like Me rather than more like Me. Don't worry. It's just a stage in the sculpting process. There are intervals in the work of precisely shaping you during which you look like a shapeless, formless lump of clay. Your old shape has been destroyed, but your new shape has not yet emerged. Don't give up. I am the Master Artist. Those are My hands you feel squeezing you and pushing you. I know exactly what I'm doing.

"Blessed one, part of the shaping is done by fire. But it is not a destroying fire; it is a cleansing fire. When you walk through it, it will not burn you. It will refine you. I am in the fire. It is going to burn away the earth stuff still clinging to you. It is going to set the work I have finished so the shape is stable."

What part of your character do you feel God is sculpting? What circumstances is He using to do His shaping?

_____

_____

_____

_____

Can you thank your Father for loving you enough to personally shape and mold you into a masterpiece of His design? Choose to thank Him for the circumstances that are forming you into His image. Write out your thanks to Him, specifically naming those circumstances.

_____

_____

_____

_____

WEEK SIX

DAY 2

YOUR WILL BE DONE

"Your kingdom come, your will be done, on earth as it is in heaven" (Matthew 6:10).

With these few words, the Prayer Teacher showed us an astounding truth about the role of prayer. Prayer is the conduit that brings the direct, intervening, specific power and provision of God into the circumstances of earth. If God's kingdom could come and His will be done apart from prayer, then why would Jesus include this petition in His pattern for prayer?

No, this is not an arm's-length, passive prayer. Rather, it is an assertive, proactive prayer. God's work is finished but prayer is how the will of God, which is fully manifest in heaven, is realized in the circumstances of earth. Prayer releases the power of God to accomplish the purposes of God.

Jesus is not teaching us to pray some generic, blanket prayer, but instead He wants us to use this prayer in every specific, minute detail of our lives. We can pray: "In this detail, Father, let Your finished work be expressed. In this situation, on this day, at this time let Your sovereign rule take direct effect. For this need, let everything available in heaven be manifested on the earth."

Jesus used strong language here. He did not hope or wish God's will would be done, but He declared that God's will be done. When, through prayer, God's people access the power and the plan of God, they can be confident that God's intervening power will take effect and His specific plan will be worked out. The working out of His plan may take a course that at times looks backward, but you can rest assured that it is always moving forward. Keep prayer flowing from start to finish.

What peace can be yours when you recognize the tool God has put at your disposal! God's work is finished and prayer will bring it into your circumstances. Blessedness means resting in His finished work, and trusting His Word that prayer will cause His plan to take effect.

What is a circumstance in your life right now? It doesn't need to be especially traumatic or difficult—just some situation in which you want the power and provision of God to be manifested. Let the Spirit of God surface in your thoughts what situation or circumstance to consider.

Set Apart

WEEK SIX

List details of that circumstance. Write down even the smallest, most insignificant details. Over each detail, claim the sovereign rule of God and the finished work of God. Over everything that comes to your mind about this situation, pray, *"Your kingdom come, your will be done."* **Then, trustfully rest.**

_____

_____

_____

_____

Willing His Will

When you discover the great truth that prayer activates the specific will of God in a situation, the thought will give you rest only if you have moved to the place of willing the will of God. Often we can have an underlying sense that God's will is something we have to bear up under or settle for. God's will, we think, is difficult and oppressive.

In Romans 12:2, Paul described God's will with three words: *good, pleasing,* and *perfect.* The Greek words used could be rendered "beneficial," "bringing pleasure," and "a perfect fit." Only when you come to know God through experience—when you have put His will to the test and have firsthand understanding that it is good—can you find rest and peace in the thought of His will being done. But the secret to experiencing God this way is that you first have to obey Him and surrender to Him in order to put His will to the test. You have to take the one step in front of you. You have to abandon the old familiar fleshways. You have to set your face like flint in the direction He is pointing you, making no provision to turn back. Only then can you say, *"Your promises have been thoroughly tested, and your servant loves them"* (Psalm 119:140).

In the Scripture, words involving the senses describe how you will know God. For example, *"Taste and see that the Lord is good"* (Psalm 34:8); *"I pray also that the eyes of your heart may be enlightened"* (Ephesians 1:18); and *"'He who has ears to hear, let him hear'"* (Mark 4:9). Why do you think God used sense-related words? I think it is because those things that you know by your senses, you know through firsthand experience. Could you, for example, describe the taste of a fresh strawberry to someone who has never tasted a fresh strawberry?

Could you describe the sound of rain or the smell of the ocean to a person who has never heard rain or smelled the ocean? What you know by means of your senses, you know because you have experienced it. So it is with the deep things of God. You must first know Him by experience. Then you will know with certainty that His will is good, pleasing, and perfect.

God reveals His will progressively. He unfolds it obedience by obedience. *"The path of the righteous is like the first gleam of dawn, shining ever brighter till the full light of day"* (Proverbs 4:18). Each obedience sets the stage for the next step. As you keep putting His promises to the test, you will discover that where there used to be hesitancy and uncertainty, there is now a settled confidence. Your steps, which started out halting and tentative, are now sure and steady. Little by little, step by step, you prove the will of God to be good, pleasing, and perfect.

Once you know for yourself that God's will is desirable, you will be able to trust that His will for all situations is equally desirable. You will learn to pray with expectant joy, "Let Your kingdom come. Let Your will be done. As in heaven, so on earth." You will rest on His will completely.

Do you know firsthand that God's will is desirable? Let the Spirit remind you of the times when you learned through experience that His plan exceeds your expectations. List them.

_____

_____

_____

_____

As you remember, let faith spring up. As you sit quietly by the still waters, let peace flow through your heart. Whatever He is calling you to now, you can trust His plan. Whatever you are praying about, you can trust His will. Write out your thoughts.

_____

_____

Set Apart

WEEK SIX

_____

_____

_____

❦ ❦ ❦

DAY 3

OUR DAILY BREAD

"Give us today our daily bread" (Matthew 6:11).

The Father wants to meet your needs. He encourages you to look to Him to supply every need that arises. He takes pleasure in supplying you with everything you need.

Why do you have needs? Why do you need shelter or food? Why do you need emotional connections with other people? Why do you need to feel a sense of purpose?

You have needs because God created you with needs. He could have made you so that your shelter is on your back, as He did the turtle. He could have made you so that you could live a solitary, isolated life. But instead, He made you with needs. The reason is so that your needs could be His entry points. Your needs will point you to His supply.

"Meet today's needs," Jesus taught us to pray. "Whatever arises today, Father, I look to You for provision."

I hear the Father whisper, "Jennifer, nothing will come into your life today for which I have not already put provision in place. Just be alert and watchful. Look to Me first; I will point you to the supply."

What an adventure it is to live this way! How it frees me from anxiety and frustration! I am learning that everything, from the major to the mundane, has been provided for by my Father. As needs arise from day to day, instead of asking, "Father, do something!" I just say, "Father, what have You already done? Where will I discover the answer You have provided? My soul rests in You, waiting patiently for Your salvation."

Please understand, God does not meet every need in the way that seems most convenient to me. If that were my measuring stick, then I would often be frustrated. But if I have given myself to Him as a living offering, then I am open for Him to meet my needs in ways that will further my understanding of Him or will advance His kingdom. You will only live a state of blessedness when you have aligned yourself with His will, so that your desire is to know Him at deeper and deeper levels. If your motivating force is to get God to perform for you—to see Him bring about your agenda—you will not find the blessedness that Jesus offers. Often, what seems an inconvenience to me puts me on the path to an encounter the Lord has arranged for me. Or, something that throws off my schedule actually provides me with information I needed—sometimes before I know I needed it.

WEEK SIX

Just Ask

"Ask and it will be given to you... For everyone who asks receives" (Matthew 7:7–8).

Jesus used a very simple form of the word *ask* in this declaration. The phrasing is like a child asking his or her parent to meet a need. Yet Jesus also said, *"Your Father knows what you need before you ask him"* (Matthew 6:8). If that's so, why ask?

Let me back up a little. The phrase the Father gave me many years ago to define my message is *the praying life*. Don't settle for "having a prayer life"—like you have a home life, and a work life, and a leisure life. Don't be satisfied with a part of your life that is set aside for prayer. Instead, "live a praying life"—a life through which prayer flows unceasingly. A praying life is a life always in active and intentional cooperation with God; a life in which an undercurrent of prayer is always present; a life of continual interaction with the spiritual realm. A praying life is a life open to the power and provision of God. A praying life focuses on, "How do I keep my life open to the Father's power?" One of the ways that you open your life to what God wants to provide is by asking!

In asking, you acknowledge the Source of everything. *"Don't be deceived, my dear brothers. Every good and perfect gift is from above, coming down from the Father of the heavenly lights, who does not change like shifting shadows"* (James 1:16–17). God instructs you to ask for what you need because this interaction keeps you aware that He is your source.

Another reason God designed prayer so that your asking releases His supply is because He wants you to see His power. If His method for meeting your needs did not engage you, you would not see His power at work. He wants you to have observable proof of His involvement in your life; He wants you to see His love for you. When you live in an "ask and receive" mode, you cannot help but be aware of—and awed by—the Father's intimate involvement in your life.

Sometimes God waits for you to ask, because until you see your need, you will not recognize His supply. He waits until you have come to the end of your own resources. He waits for you to turn to Him as the one and only Source.

Remember when you unlocked the meaning of James 4:1–3 in Week Five. This passage includes this statement: *"You do not have because you do not ask God."* Then James goes on to say: *"When you ask, you do not receive, because you ask with wrong motives, that you may spend what you get on your pleasures."*

Does that mean God does not want to give you anything that is for your pleasure? Does it mean that He is always weighing our motives and if there is any hint of our delight in them, God will withhold? Not at all. God loves to delight you. But He will withhold what you ask for when it would further your weakness rather than bringing you deeper into relationship with Him.

My friend illustrated this kind of love in a conversation recently. She has a daughter whom she loves, who is currently living a rebellious and self-destructive lifestyle. My friend told me that her daughter asked her for money, and she refused to give it. Her refusal came not because she wanted to withhold money from her daughter. In fact, it was difficult for her to refuse. Her refusal came because she knew that the money would be spent in ways that would harm her daughter. Out of her love for her daughter she refused her daughter's request.

So it is with God. He knows what will keep you from your true destiny and lead you away from His path for you. Sometimes the things we ask for may seem good, even spiritual, but God knows how they will really affect us. For example, imagine that a woman asks God for more fruit in ministry, but God seems to withhold it. Could it be that God knows that, at this point in her development, more tangible "success" in her ministry would cause her to be filled with pride? In such a case, God wants to deal with some flesh-issues before He gives more fruit in ministry. Or, suppose a single person asks God for a mate and God seems to withhold the answer. Could it be that God knows that right now a mate, would distract the person from his or her wholehearted pursuit of Him? God knows what He is doing, and you can trust Him. You can trust that His motivation is your best interest.

I love to say yes to my children. I love to give them what they ask for. In fact, there are only two reasons I will ever say no. One is if I don't have the resources. The other is if I think it will not ultimately be in their best interest. God loves to say yes to us. He is never short of resources, so the only reason He might not give us exactly what we ask for is because He knows it would not be in our best interest. It would not bring into our lives what we probably think it would bring.

Blessedness comes in trusting His love for you and His wisdom. Peace is yours when you know that He will never withhold from you something that would truly make your life more complete. When you are living in a flow of prayer—a praying life—you can always know: "God will meet my need in the right way at the right time with the right resources. If it is best for my need to be fully met today, then it will be."

Ask God for what you need. State your trust in Him to supply your need(s) in the right time and in the right way. Write out your thoughts.

_____

_____

_____

_____

DAY 4

FORGIVEN

"Forgive us our debts, as we also have forgiven our debtors" (Matthew 6:12).

Jesus, in His prayer outline, tied together the forgiveness we receive from the Father and the forgiveness we offer to others. One is the outgrowth of the other. Because we have received forgiveness, we extend forgiveness. Blessed are the merciful, for they will be shown mercy.

The word translated "forgive" means "to send off" or "to send away." The act of forgiving separates the sin from the one who sinned. It "sends away" the sin, with its penalty and its attendant guilt. This transaction was pictured in the Old Testament by the sacrificial system. The guilty person made a sin offering or guilt offering with an unblemished animal from his own livestock. Before killing the animal, he laid his hands on the animal. He leaned into the animal with all his weight. This symbolized laying his sins on the animal; the animal was bearing the "weight" of his sins. Then he killed the animal, recognizing that the wages of sin is death. As that person leaned his weight upon the sacrificial animal, the Lord declared, *""It will be accepted on his behalf to make atonement for him"""* (Leviticus 1:4). The sin was separated from the one who sinned because it had been placed on the sacrifice.

The forgiveness we receive from the Father is not a passive act but instead a costly transaction. Your forgiveness and my forgiveness from the Father is available because *"the LORD has laid on him the iniquity of us all"* (Isaiah 53:6). Do you see? God separated you from your sin. He took the sin off of you and placed it on the Son. He sent your sin away. The One who knew no sin became sin for us. It is finished and settled.   Lean the weight of your sin on Him who took your sin to the Cross. You are forgiven. How much He loves you! The act of sacrifice—the sacrifice of the Son and the sacrifice of the Father—was not a generic, impersonal action, but a specific, directed, intimate action on your behalf. The Father's love for you is as personal as if you were His only love.

Have you received His love fully in accepting His forgiveness? Or do you continue to hold on to guilt and shame? Do you hang your head in His presence? Or have you discovered Him as *"the One who lifts my head"* (Psalm 3:3 NASB)?

Are you struggling with guilt for past sins? Right now, lean the weight of that sin on Him. See in your heart that He took it upon Himself to the Cross. Look at the scene until the truth of it settles in.

Name the past sins that He bore the weight of for you. Write them down. Let them go.

_____

_____

_____

_____

❧ ❧ ❧

A Forgiven Forgiver

"And when you stand praying, if you hold anything against anyone, forgive him, so that your Father in heaven may forgive you your sins" (Mark 11:25).

Choosing not to forgive others is closing the door to God's forgiveness. This does not mean that when you do not forgive, God withholds His forgiveness as a punishment. It does not mean that you earn your forgiveness by forgiving others. If this were so, it would directly contradict the entire gospel message. Your forgiveness is a settled matter, settled at the Cross. Christ's death in your place fulfilled your obligation and erased your debt. God will not go back on His Word. Yet, this concept tying your forgiveness of those who wrong you to God's forgiveness of you is repeated and emphasized by Jesus. In His inaugural address, he said, *"For if you forgive men when they sin against you, your heavenly Father will also forgive you. But if you do not forgive men their sins, your Father will not forgive your sins"* (Matthew 6:14–15). So we must come to an understanding of what He means.

Foundational to this understanding is the recognition of how much God has forgiven you. If you were the only person ever to commit a sin, Jesus would still have died for you. It still would have taken His death on the Cross to pay for your sins alone. When He died on the Cross, it was for your sins. The Father has forgiven you more than you will ever be called upon to forgive any other person. The cost of His forgiveness is a higher price than you will ever have to pay. No matter what anyone has ever done to you, that person's sin against you does not come close to the measure of your sins against God.

Second, you, on your own, have neither the inclination nor the ability to forgive. You are just the conduit of God's forgiveness. Christ living in you does His work. Holding on to anger cuts off the flow of His power through you. It clogs the channel through which His love flows.

Third, understand that when Jesus said, *"so that your Father in heaven may forgive you your sins,"* He did not refer to the action of forgiving—which Jesus knew would be finished at the Cross—but instead referred to having His forgiveness in your experience. He wants forgiveness to move from being an abstract theological concept to being your truth. Deliberately nursing a grievance, holding it close and giving it nourishment, keeps the reality of the Father's forgiveness from you. When you choose to hold on to anger or bitterness, you refuse to let go of a sin—the sin of unforgiveness. It is the confessing and turning from a sin that brings the Father's forgiveness into your experience.

The Scripture tells us that deliberate unforgiveness gives the enemy an opening. Paul wrote: *"What I have forgiven—if there was anything to forgive— I have forgiven in the sight of Christ for your sake, in order that Satan might not outwit us. For we are not unaware of his schemes"* (2 Corinthians 2:10–11). As you forgive those who have wronged you, you close the door to Satan's schemes, and you open the door to the power of God.

You can live in the state of blessedness that comes from forgiving others and letting go of the turmoil that anger and resentment bring to your emotions. When you believe what God says about the high price of your forgiveness, you will be ready to forgive anybody anything. Forgive and let the peace of Christ stand guard over your heart.

What or whom are you struggling to forgive?

Do you want to be free of the bitterness and the anger? If you do, ask the Father to do His work in you and through you? Write it out.

Be patient with the process as the Father heals. You are in His hands. Don't take the burden on yourself.

The Law in Your Heart

You were not designed to carry anger and bitterness. It weighs you down and holds you back. Because the Father loves you, He does not want you bearing a burden that is not yours to bear.

When Jesus took on the weight of your sin and carried it to the Cross, He also carried the sins committed against you. When you insist on holding on to the hurts inflicted on you, you deny the power of His crucifixion. He died for sinners, for the ungodly. *"You see, at just the right time, when we were still power-less, Christ died for the ungodly.... God demonstrates his own love for us in this: While we were still sinners, Christ died for us"* (Romans 5:6–8). Is your offender a sinner? Christ died for his sins. Is your offender ungodly? Christ died for her. Extend grace—the same grace that God extended to you.

Not only did He carry your sin, but He bore the weight of your grief and your sorrows. He bore the hurt of the sins committed against you. Just as you have leaned the weight of your sins on Him, now lean the weight of your grief and your sorrow on Him. Let Him pick it up and carry it. It is too heavy for you.

By bearing the weight of your own hurt, you allow the offense to continue and to multiply its effect on you. You may be passing the hurt along to others in your life. The offense grows and spreads. *"See to it that no one misses the grace of God and that no bitter root grows up to cause trouble and defile many"* (Hebrews 12:15). If bitterness is allowed to take root in you, it will begin to grow fruit. Your actions, words, attitudes, and responses will be bitter fruit growing from a bitter root. It will create bitterness in those who are exposed to it. One offense can poison many people, even spreading from generation to generation. Do you really want to enable your offender to have access to so many lives? Wouldn't it be better to forgive and let your life produce the fruit of the Spirit instead?

WEEK SIX

DAY 5

LEAD US NOT INTO TEMPTATION

"And lead us not into temptation, but deliver us from the evil one" (Matthew 6:13).

"'Why are you sleeping?' [Jesus] asked them. 'Get up and pray so that you will not fall into temptation'" (Luke 22:46). The word translated "temptation" also means "testing, trial, proving." During those emotionally charged hours before His arrest, Jesus urgently reminded His disciples to strengthen themselves through prayer against the onslaught of testing headed their way. That openness to the flow of God's power and provision (prayer) would provide the victory in the moment of testing. When the moment came for proving what was on the inside, the battle the disciples faced could have been won in the prayer that preceded it.

At least twice during His prayer vigil Jesus admonished His disciples with these words. Don't you think that this gives us some insight into the spiritual battle in which Jesus was engaged during His Gethsemane hours? The moment was approaching for which His whole purpose in coming to earth would be put to the test. His mission would be tested and proven. Jesus, during His period of agonized praying, received from the Father the strength, assurance, endurance, courage, and confidence to face the temptation—more accurately, the trial—and not fall. His mental, emotional, and spiritual serenity throughout His crucifixion experience was birthed in the hours of prayer and the life of prayer that preceded it.

> *Praying, true praying, costs an outlay of serious attention and time, which flesh and blood do not relish. Few are made of such strong fiber that they will make a costly outlay when surface work will pass just as well in the market.*
>
> *To be little with God is to be little for God.... It takes good time for the full flow of God into the spirit. Short devotions cut the pipe of God's full flow.... We live shabbily because we pray meanly.*
> —E. M. Bounds, *Power Through Prayer*

Did the Father lead Him into that trial? The record of Scripture is clear. Evil persons with evil intent made and carried out their evil plans. Satan, in fact, orchestrated the events. Yet all of the decisions and actions lined up with the timetable and the purposes God had laid out and announced throughout history (see Acts 2:23). Jesus, doing only what the Father showed Him to do, found Himself in the midst of the ultimate testing. His praying life, however,

Set Apart

prepared Him and focused Him so that in the moment of testing He did not fall.

He had already taught His disciples to pray, *"Lead us not into temptation."* Let me paraphrase for you what I think that petition means: "When my path leads me through times of proving—authenticating what is inside me—hold me so that I do not fall. When Satan asks and receives permission to sift me like wheat, keep me from falling into his trap." Living in this attitude of dependence upon Him readies you for the circumstances that take you by surprise, giving Him the opportunity to prove His sufficiency.

This prayer, then, does not surface from a desire to hide from any difficulty or challenge. The person who prays this prayer in the context of a praying life asks that any oncoming test will be one that will move her closer to her goal— the goal she shares with the Father—to be conformed to the image of the Son. Until this is the focus and the intent of her life, the testings that come her way will fail to yield that "weight of glory" they were meant to produce.

> My goal is God Himself, not joy nor peace;
> Nor even blessing, but Himself, my God.
> 'Tis His to lead me there, not mine, but His…
> "At any cost, dear Lord, by any road."
> —Frederick Brook

Are you spending the time in prayer that will prepare you for the testing circumstances that are sure to come your way?

_____

What do you need to do to make prayer a daily priority?

_____

_____

_____

_____

CLOSING PRAYER

BE BLESSED

As you conclude this study, my prayer is that you have come to know King Jesus as your Ruler and your Rabbi. I pray that:

- You have looked into the heart of God and surrendered your heart for Him to shape and mold into a perfect expression of His.

- You have seen that holiness is the root of happiness. You have embraced your position as one set apart—taken from common use and declared holy to the Lord.

- You have discovered that the living law, engraved on your heart, is becoming your natural response and inclination. Jesus, the Law Himself—the fullness of God embodied—is living in you and working through you.

✎ You are living on the earth, but dwelling in the kingdom.

✎ You are discovering daily more of the blessedness of kingdom living. You are fully supplied within and so progressively less controlled by outward circumstances.

✎ That which you first heard as command, you now hear as promise. *"You shall be holy, for I am holy."*

✎ That which was once impossible to obey is becoming impossible to disobey.

Blessed are you!

Set Apart

New Hope® Publishers is a division of WMU®, an international organization that challenges Christian believers to understand and be radically involved in God's mission. For more information about WMU, go to www.wmu.com. More information about New Hope books may be found at www.newhopepublishers.com. New Hope books may be purchased at your local bookstore.

If you've been blessed by this book, we would like to hear your story.
The publisher and author welcome your comments and
suggestions at: newhopereader@wmu.org.

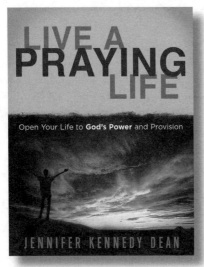
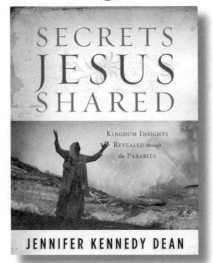
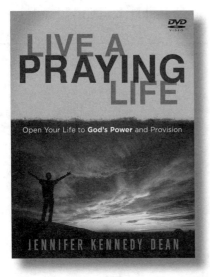
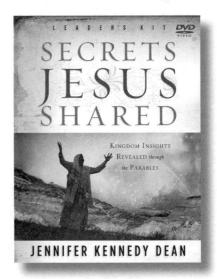